The
Secret Betrayal of
Britain's Wartime Allies

Regards

Jim Auton.

"How, after the fall of Warsaw, any responsible statesman could trust any Russian Communist further than he could kick him, passes the comprehension of ordinary men".

(MRAF Sir John Slessor, Commander of the airmen who flew to Warsaw during the 1944 uprising).

The
Secret Betrayal of
Britain's Wartime Allies

The appeasement of Stalin and its post-war consequences

Jim Auton MBE

Pen & Sword
AVIATION

First published in Great Britain in 2014 by
PEN & SWORD AVIATION
An imprint of
Pen & Sword Books Ltd
47 Church Street
Barnsley
South Yorkshire
S70 2AS

Copyright © Jim Auton MBE 2014

ISBN 978 1 78383 158 6

Pen & Sword Books Ltd incorporates the Imprints of Pen & Sword Aviation, Pen & Sword Family History, Pen & Sword Maritime, Pen & Sword Military, Pen & Sword Discovery, Wharncliffe Local History, Wharncliffe True Crime, Wharncliffe Transport, Pen & Sword Select, Pen & Sword Military Classics, Leo Cooper, The Praetorian Press, Remember When, Seaforth Publishing and Frontline Publishing

Printing in England by Anthony Rowe UK.

For a complete list of Pen & Sword titles please contact
PEN & SWORD BOOKS LIMITED
47 Church Street, Barnsley, South Yorkshire, S70 2AS, England
E-mail: enquiries@pen-and-sword.co.uk
Website: www.pen-and-sword.co.uk.

Contents

To the memory of brave men and women of wartime underground resistance forces and their forgotten compatriots who served in the British Armed Forces.

Publisher's Note.
This book is based on the personal experiences of the author, his fellow combatants and his colleagues. Where the publishers are unable to find historical evidence to support certain sections of the author's work notes are provided to indicate the fact.

Acknowledgements

I am grateful to the following kind friends who encouraged me to write this book about the Polish, Czechoslovak and other airmen who served under them, and also about the partisans who were supported by the Allied air forces in enemy-occupied territory:

Air Chief Marshal Sir Frederick Rosier, commander of Polish fighter squadrons;

Wing Commander Cecil Harper, Senior Operations Officer of the Balkans Air Force;

Bickham Sweet-Escott, business colleague and Head of SOE Polish and Balkan sections;

Group Captain Ken Bachelor, commander of 138 Squadron RAF at Tempsford;

Group Captain Ron Hockey, commander of 138 and 161 Squadrons RAF;

Colonel Wojchiech Borzobohaty, Armia Krajowa area commander.

I also acknowledge encouragement and help received from the following:

former Czech and Polish ambassadors (ex-partisans) and defence attachés;

Mr Skolimowski, former Polish Consul General;

fellow veterans of 205 Group RAF;

fellow members of the Armia Krajowa Association in Warsaw;

fellow members of the Air Bridge Association;

fellow pilots of the Czechoslovak Air Force (I am an honorary pilot);

Colonel Pavlik of SVAZ LECU Pilots' Association in Prague;

General Spacek and others of the Czechoslovak Legionnaires Association;

General Siska and others of the Czechoslovak ex-RAF Association in Prague; General Petrak MBE MC, my liaison officer in Slovakia;

Professor Popovich, Veterans' Council Chairman, Transcarpathian Region, Ukraine;

Wojciech Borzobohaty Junior.

CHAPTER ONE

Although the massive slaughter of the Second World War was barely over, we already faced the threat of another deadly conflict. The long Cold War had begun.

Getting out of the car, I turned up the collar of my thick overcoat against the biting chill of autumn and shoved my hands deep into my pockets. I knew that our airmen's graves lay in the far corner of Poland's vast war cemetery and, as I skirted around the multitude of Russian and Polish soldiers' graves, my feelings turned from sadness to bitterness. I said to Zak, my Polish companion, 'What a bloody awful waste of lives!' He sorrowfully shook his head and muttered, 'And was it all worth it? Our people are scarcely any better off now under Russian occupation than we were under the Germans. In fact, we had more food then.'

It was late afternoon and I hoped the light would not fade before I managed to locate the particular graves that I wanted to record with my little pocket camera. On reaching the air force section, I walked quickly along the rows of graves, photographing the headstones of friends who had flown to Poland with me from our wartime base in Italy. Kneeling to press a little wooden remembrance cross into the grave of Squadron Leader Liversidge, my former flight commander, I found the ground was like concrete. No doubt the Poles did their best to maintain the site properly but, as grass and flowers did not grow well in the harsh Polish climate, the war graves looked rather shabby and forlorn compared with those in the west. Zak watched me planting the cross and said, 'Our Polish veterans have marked his crash site with a plaque in Krakow. I can show you where it is tomorrow, if you like.' I explained that I was committed to a business visit to the Huta Baildon steelworks in Katowice and said, 'Show me when I come to Krakow again. I will make sure I am not so busy next time.'

As we searched along the rows of headstones, I saw that a couple of elderly women in drab peasant-style clothes and well-worn leather boots were sweeping fallen leaves off the gravel pathways with birch brooms. I offered them some Polish money and said, 'Take good care of these graves for me; these men were my friends.' The women looked startled. I spoke in German because I knew that Poles of their age in southern Poland understood that language. Now, at the height of the Cold War, every Pole was deeply suspicious of strangers. I saw the anxiety in the women's eyes and hastened to assure them that I was not trying to trick them. 'I am not a communist. I was one of the English airmen who flew to Warsaw during the 1944 Uprising.' As I switched into my primitive Polish, they nodded, 'Da, powstanie.' Every Pole knew about our pathetic efforts to support the tragic Warsaw Uprising in 1944. The women grasped my hands and kissed my fingers before taking the Polish money and stuffing it away under their voluminous skirts. They immediately stopped work on the paths and began vigorously to clear dead leaves off the airmen's graves while I tried to take photographs without getting the women in the pictures. Zak called out to me, 'Is this one of yours? I don't think he is on our list of Warsaw casualties.' I noted the name Leo on the gravestone and the date, 20 August 1944. I said, 'I don't remember him. I will try to find out something about him in London when I get back.' By the time I had photographed the graves of men from my old squadron, I was feeling increasingly resentful and depressed. I said to Zak, 'I am worried about the trouble with Russia. I think it will not be long before the shooting starts again and next time it will be a damn sight worse than before.'

As we trudged back to the cemetery gates, I saw a few shabbily dressed old people placing glass jars containing flickering candle stubs on private graves of Polish pilots. A couple of nuns, busily polishing a large tomb, stopped work and hid when they saw us approaching. We got into my car and I said to Zak, 'I don't know about you, but I hate graveyards and I'm bloody frozen stiff.' He said, 'What we need are a couple of vodkas.' Zak had been a sixteen-year-old wartime partisan. In his spare time he now recorded the sites of shot-down Royal Air Force planes and the names of casualties. In addition to my lucrative sales activities in capitalist countries, I had recently started visiting countries behind the mysterious Iron Curtain. Although ostensibly engaged solely on promoting East-West trade, I secretly undertook other activities such as research into our wartime air force actions over the lands that became Soviet satellites at the end of the war.

The name Leo puzzled me. I thought I knew the identity of every airman shot down over Poland. I would certainly not have forgotten such an uncommon name. I painstakingly searched through official records and discovered that he was killed during an air attack while he was a prisoner of war at the notorious Auschwitz death camp. I was determined to learn more. I had not previously known of British prisoners at Auschwitz. If I failed to get further details in England, I might seek Polish permission to research the extensive German documents at Auschwitz. I knew that the Poles had preserved the concentration camp in its hideous wartime condition as a grim reminder of Nazi atrocities.

Further research revealed that Leo had been an air gunner in a crew of sergeants, whose Halifax bomber of Number 35 Squadron RAF took off from Linton-on-Ouse in mid-August 1942. It was the squadron's first flight as Pathfinders (target markers). The authorities chose Flensburg as the intended target, because they mistakenly assumed that inexperienced crews might locate it easily in the dark. However, very few, if any, aircraft dropped their bombs anywhere near the target and Leo's crew actually dropped theirs twenty-five miles away in Denmark. Automatic photographs taken by several other crews showed that their bombs fell at distances varying from seven to twenty-one miles from the target and later reconnaissance photographs revealed that Flensburg was undamaged. Leo's plane did not return to its base and, in due course, the International Red Cross reported that the crew were prisoners of war in Germany.

The abortive raid on Flensburg was typical of Britain's bomber activity at that stage of the war. The British authorities were fully aware that bomber crews were seldom able to find their targets and bomb accurately in the dark, but there were 'good reasons' for repeatedly sending men on perilous flights simply to make holes in the ground. For the past year the Germans had been relentlessly beating back the Red Army and Stalin was continually goading Churchill, our war leader, to open a second front in the west instead of 'leaving the Russian troops to do all the fighting'. Churchill was well aware that the western Allies were incapable of launching a successful ground offensive on the European continent at that time, so to counter Stalin's jibes he repeatedly claimed that bombers of the Royal Air Force were indeed taking the pressure off the Red Army by 'mercilessly pounding the Germans every night'. The British authorities feared that Stalin might give up the fight, capitulate to the Germans and allow them to transfer their full force to the west. Stalin, therefore, had to be appeased and encouraged to fight on at all costs, so the sacrifice of bomber crews who had no hope of locating their targets in the dark was a callous expedient. It would be many months before our night-bomber force became an effective weapon of war instead of a mere propaganda tool.

In April 1942 a shocking example of wasted airmen and planes had occurred when twelve Lancaster bombers were sent in daylight to make a low-level attack on the MAN diesel engine factory at Augsburg in southern Germany. Seven of the twelve bombers were shot down and all the others were damaged. Seventeen bombs hit the target, but five failed to explode and disruption of the factory's production of submarine engines was minimal. Our official propaganda-mongers acclaimed the raid as a great achievement but, in truth, it was nothing more than a ghastly and expensive blunder. We airmen were, of course, unaware of the truth. We blindly obeyed orders from our superiors no matter how dangerous or ridiculous some of those orders seemed to be. By the time the United States Army Air Forces began their belated strategic bombing offensive from British bases, the Royal Air Force had switched from suicidal daylight attacks to night bombing. Disregarding British warnings, the Americans embarked upon a campaign of daytime bombing. They assumed that their heavily-armed Liberator and Flying Fortress bombers, flying in tight formations, would be able to battle their way through enemy opposition. They were mistaken and their casualty rate was enormous until eventually their Mustang fighters, fitted with overload tanks and British Rolls-Royce Merlin engines, were able to escort the bombers to their targets.

Continuing my investigations of Sergeant Leo, I unearthed some surprising facts. During an air raid, he was in a working party alongside foreign slave workers in the German Bunawerke (synthetic rubber works) adjacent to the Auschwitz death camp. Although the Poles had repeatedly urged the western allies to bomb the death camp and destroy the crematoria, their pleas were rejected because such actions were not regarded as legitimate acts of war. However, on 20 August 1944, over one hundred bombers of the United States Fifteenth Air Force attacked the nearby factory. All the bombers flew from bases in the Foggia region of Italy where my own squadron was located. Some of the planes actually came from the Amendola airstrip that we shared with the Americans. During the raid a few prisoners were killed by bombs inadvertently dropped on the death camp. Other innocent prisoners, like Leo, were killed by bombs dropped on the targeted factory. The attacking airmen could not have guessed that in bombing the Auschwitz factory they were slaughtering Allied prisoners of war and innocent slave workers from the death camp. After the war, some of the Auschwitz survivors were allowed to settle in England and I mentioned Leo's name to women who were in the camp at the time of his death. Although none could recall a man with his name, they all remembered how British airmen risked being shot by armed guards for throwing bread over the electrified wire into the compound of the half-starved women. One woman showed me a flying badge obtained from a British airman at Auschwitz. She never knew his name. From the day when I first discovered Leo's grave in Poland, it took me many months of painstaking research to uncover the circumstances that led to his death. Incidentally, Leo was a sergeant when he was shot down and the air force promoted him twice while he was a prisoner of war, so he was a warrant officer when he died. I wonder what happened to his 'back pay'. I recall that my own overdue pay mysteriously disappeared while I lay wounded in a British military hospital for three months.

Leo and his friends were shot down on 18 August 1942 and on the following day the disastrous landing of around 6,000 Canadian and British troops took place on the French coast at Dieppe. The troops were put ashore at an entirely unsuitable location in the face of fierce enemy opposition and most of them were either killed or captured within the first few hours. Canadian troops suffered the greatest losses and German flak shot down scores of our planes. After the war some commentators assumed that the Dieppe debacle was due to the ignorance and incompetence of the military planners. A more likely explanation is that it was, like the futile Royal Air Force raids of the time, a deliberate and deadly propaganda exercise intended to pacify Stalin. The worst examples of blundering incompetence were yet to come at places like Arnhem. At the time the British public were unaware of the extent of the Dieppe fiasco, but the Canadian sergeant pilots at my flying school knew of it and that may have accounted for their truculent attitude towards the authorities. Saluting of officers had been discontinued on the air base, but I often saw how the Canadians tricked the officers. When they saw an officer approaching, they braced themselves and raised their right arms smartly. The officer's automatic reaction was to salute, but the Canadian airmen merely readjusted their caps or scratched their ears. They then adopted a mock-bewildered expression as though unable to understand why the officer had saluted them. The Canadians' truculent attitude and intolerance of unnecessary 'bullshit' soon spread to other aircrew personnel.

After visiting the Huta Baildon steelworks I drove to Warsaw, booked into the dilapidated Grand Hotel and telephoned Metalexport, the state trading corporation, to arrange business discussions for the following day. Then, having nothing else to do, I wandered through the war-torn streets of the city into the ancient Stare Miasto area that the poverty-stricken Poles had lovingly rebuilt with the aid of ancient maps, paintings and photographs. In the old town square I admired the restored buildings and remembered that, in 1944, the square had been one of the drop zones where, in the darkness, our planes had released parachute containers of supplies for the underground resistance army. As I stood reminiscing about my wartime flights and wondering if I should risk using my camera, I became aware of a man watching me intently. I knew that the communist secret police kept foreigners under surveillance and I naturally tried to avoid their attention. It was a chilly afternoon, so I slunk into the nearby smoke-filled Krokodil bar and settled down with a glass of miod (honey wine) – the speciality of the house. I soon noticed that the man whom I had tried to avoid outside had followed me into the bar and was obviously looking for me. He sat down at the same table, leaned across to me and said something in Polish that I could not understand. I replied in my primitive Polish, 'Sorry, I not understand.' He asked, 'Deutsch?' I replied in German that I understood German but that I was English. He beamed, '*Gut. Sprechen wir Deutsch.*' He explained that he had noticed me examining wall plaques commemorating people the Germans had gunned down in the streets as reprisals whenever Polish resistance forces killed Warsaw's hated occupiers. He had only met one English airman before and that was during the war. He was keen to learn about my flights in support of the 1944 Uprising, but I wanted him to tell me about the English airman. From his coat pocket, he fished out a Cross of Valour that he had won during the uprising and told me, 'The Englishman got this too. He was a lieutenant in the Armia Krajowa (underground army).' 'What was his name and what did he look like?' I asked. He replied, 'I only saw him a couple of times, so I cannot remember him very well. I think he was rather arrogant, not very tall and with a snub-nosed face. I believe he was wounded in the leg, but not killed. I heard men say his name. It sounded like Vard, but I do not know how to spell it.' I was intrigued. I would have to search my records for a Ward. I could not recall anyone of that name who might have survived being shot down over Warsaw. I asked, 'Have you any friends – other veterans – who might know something about the airman called Ward?' He replied, 'If you want to meet some of my friends, I will bring them here tomorrow. I am sure they will like to meet you too. We will wait for you outside the Krokodil at three o'clock.' I said, 'Don't stay outside in the cold. Wait inside and let me pay the bill. This place is not expensive by English standards.' I knew that Metalexport stopped work at two o'clock, so I would be free in plenty of time for the rendezvous after a quick snack at the Grand Hotel.

My new Polish friends were waiting on the pavement near the Krokodil when I arrived. There were four of them. Unfortunately, none of them knew much about Ward, but they had all been in Warsaw's Old Town when our planes arrived. I invited the men to come with me into the bar where I ordered a bottle of the delicious honey wine and they taught me '*Dod na*', the Polish encouragement to drink up. They mentioned that, as war veterans' organizations were banned by the communist government, they had formed a ramblers' club, which was the same thing in disguise and they invited me to their next meeting. The chance encounter with the man whom I had tried to avoid in case he was a secret policeman was to lead to many years of close friendship with hundreds of war veterans behind the Iron Curtain. During the height of the Cold War, citizens behind the Iron Curtain came under immediate suspicion by the police if found to be associating unofficially with western foreigners. Consequently, my meetings with my new-found friends had to be 'cloak and dagger' affairs conducted in private houses or in the sort of small bars not usually frequented by foreigners like me.

CHAPTER TWO

In the drab surroundings behind the Iron Curtain I was conspicuous in my expensive western clothes, so I attempted to merge into the background by disguising myself in cheap Polish clothes. I will return to the subject of my disguise later, but meanwhile I want to continue with the history of Ward, the British airman. I was particularly interested in him because he had been fighting against the German occupiers of Warsaw while I was flying through a hail of gunfire, seeking a suitable place in the burning city to drop my load of guns and ammunition for the Polish underground army. John Ward, the son of a Birmingham metalworker, was nineteen years old when he joined the Royal Air Force in 1937. Eight months after the start of the Second World War, he was flying as a wireless operator/air gunner in single-engined Fairey Battle bombers of Number 226 Squadron, RAF. The slow Fairey Battles were widely regarded as flying coffins because so many of them were shot down on every daytime bombing raid. On 10 May 1940, plane K9183 took off from the squadron's temporary airfield at Reims in France. Ward's fellow crew members were Flying Officer Cameron, an Australian pilot, and Sergeant Hart, the observer, whose duties included navigation and bomb-aiming. Their target was a bridge near Diekirch in Luxembourg. At the time Ward was an aircraftman first class (one rank from the bottom) and his pay was about two pounds per week. Flying Officer Cameron was attempting an extremely low-level attack on the bridge when his plane was brought down by machine-gun fire. German troops rushed towards the crashed plane and Ward, who was not too seriously injured, shouted a warning that there were bombs on board. The Germans hesitated long enough for Ward to burn some documents and set fire to the plane. He then admitted that there were actually no bombs on the plane and the Germans, looking irate over being fooled, took the airmen into custody. An ambulance conveyed the crew to a hospital where the pilot died during an operation on his injured arm, part of which had been shot off. Ward and the sergeant observer received treatment for their injuries in military hospitals at Trier and Oberursel. It was six months before they eventually reached a prison camp.

During Ward's time in hospitals, he began learning German in preparation for an escape attempt. After spending a few weeks at Stalag Luft I (Barth), he was sent to a labour camp in Upper Silesia where he became an interpreter with a prisoners' working party. While planning to escape he obtained civilian clothes, maps and a compass by bartering goods with local people. In April 1941 when, incidentally, I was just starting my training as a pupil pilot, Ward was in charge of a group of about twenty prisoners clearing trees in woods near Lissa, Germany. He was wearing civilian clothes under his uniform and, at about 2 o'clock in the afternoon, he slipped away from the working party, unobserved by the two German guards. After running a couple of miles through woodland, he hid his uniform under a pile of leaves and proceeded eastwards at night, avoiding built-up areas and hiding in the woods in the daytime.

After three days he reached Gostyn where, under cover of darkness, he entered the railway yards with the intention of climbing into a freight car going east. By the dim light of a match, he was trying to read the destination label on the side of a wagon when two railway policemen pounced on him and demanded his identity documents. As he was unable to produce any documents, he was arrested and taken to the local police station where he was searched and his prisoner of war tag was discovered. Under interrogation he told the truth about his escape and asked to be returned to the labour camp. The police told him that a senior official would deal with him the following day and that he would probably be shot. He was locked in a small cell at the back of the building, where he was to remain overnight. The only window was criss-crossed with strands of barbed wire. During the night he broke the barbed wire by bending it back and forth until he made a hole big enough to climb through into a yard. To his dismay, he saw that a ten-foot-high wall topped by broken glass enclosed the yard and an armed sentry guarded the open gateway. Fortunately, it was a fairly dark night, so he quietly approached the sentry and thumped him violently on the head with a brick that he had picked up in the yard. The sentry, who was wearing a soft forage cap, slumped silently to the ground and Ward sprinted through the gate and ran away as fast as he could. He knew that recapture now would mean certain death, so he kept off the roads, walked across fields during the hours of darkness and hid during daylight. The police had taken his compass and maps during his interrogation at the police station, and he had nothing to eat or drink, so he risked calling at isolated farmyards where he sought shelter during the daytime and scavenged small amounts of animal feed.

Around 27 April 1941, he reached the German area of Sifradz and contacted men of the Polish secret underground resistance forces who, after a thorough interrogation, provided him with a set of forged papers. He was now able to travel to Warsaw and meet up with senior officials of the Polish Armia Krajowa. The Armia Krajowa, or AK, was the world's largest and most efficient secret resistance force during the Second World War. Led by professional senior officers, its main activities were sabotage and the killing of German soldiers. The British were aware of the existence of the AK, but were only prepared to support it with a few air-dropped weapons for sabotage purposes. The British Foreign Secretary feared that any larger amount of support might enable the Poles to attack the Soviet Russians, who had illegally occupied the eastern half of Poland in 1939, while the Germans were attacking the western half. Before Hitler's invasion of the Soviet Union in 1941, the AK had been principally engaged on sabotaging huge trainloads of vital material that Stalin willingly supplied to Hitler's Germany. At that time Britain had stood alone and helpless in the face of the overwhelming might of Hitler's forces. The President of the United States assured his voters that 'no American boys would be sent to fight in a foreign war' and our newspapers reported that the Molotov/Ribbentrop Pact signified an alliance between Stalin and Hitler. It seemed that our Prime Minister Churchill, allegedly described by the US President as 'drunk half the time', was the only politician confident that Britain could survive. The outlook was bleak until Hitler sealed Germany's fate by foolishly attacking the Soviet Union and then declaring war on the United States after the Japanese had bombed the American naval base at Pearl Harbor. Britain now had the support of two potentially powerful, albeit formerly reluctant, combatants.

In Warsaw, Ward discovered that most Poles hated the Russians and Germans in equal measure. Although the Russians were now officially described as 'Britain's gallant allies' and our Prime Minister's wife led a lively campaign to raise money from the British public to aid the Soviet Union's war effort, the Poles always referred to the Russians coldly as just 'allies of our allies'. Ward soon became safely integrated into Warsaw's population. He maintained close links to the underground forces and obtained work repairing electrical apparatus. By the end of July 1944 the German forces were hastily retreating through Warsaw after the Red Army had beaten them back from the gates of Moscow and Stalingrad. The Germans had already evacuated their administrative and medical personnel, and some of their dispirited Hungarian troops deserted after quietly disposing of their small arms to eager Polish buyers in the street markets. As hordes of defeated German troops retreated through Warsaw with their horse-drawn transport and looted farm animals, the time seemed appropriate for the Poles to seize control of their capital city and foil Stalin's plan to install a communist puppet government. Warsaw's Poles were intent on establishing a working civil administration before the imminently expected arrival of the Red Army.

At five o'clock in the afternoon of 1 August 1944, the Armia Krajowa began a concerted attack on the German occupying troops. The Poles had enough supplies to last only a few days, but were initially confident that they could hold out until the Red Army arrived. The Russian troops were already in Warsaw's suburb of Praga on the other side of the river Vistula, and the low level of the river would present no obstacle to the Russians who were experts at crossing rivers. After several days of successful attacks on the Germans, the Poles began to run short of supplies and, when their appeal to the Red Army for support failed, they sent urgent radio messages asking the British government for assistance. Disappointingly, their pleas to the British also brought no support. The Poles decided that if Ward would send messages describing the serious situation in Warsaw, the British authorities would surely believe him and react favourably. Members of the Armia Krajowa's high command told Ward, 'We want you to contact the British government's ministers and important military people.' Ward protested that he did not know any important people in England. The Poles told him, 'Be assured that we do know all the right people. You just have to send our messages under your own name.'

When Ward began to despatch radio messages to London on behalf of the beleaguered Armia Krajowa, the recipients asked him for proof of his claim to be an English airman. He gave them not only his name, rank, number and place of birth, but also his mother's maiden name, father's first name and his parents' address in Birmingham.

As the situation in Warsaw deteriorated, the Poles pleaded repeatedly for help from the nearby Red Army commander, General Rokossowski, who had halted his advance on instructions from Stalin. It was Stalin's intention to allow all traces of the Polish anti-communist authorities to be crushed by the Germans before his troops entered the city. In response to the British government's suggestions that the Red Army should assist the Armia Krajowa, Stalin branded the Warsaw insurgents as terrorists. He referred to the uprising as a 'reckless adventure' and refused to be associated with it. Molotov, his foreign secretary, informed Clark Kerr, the British Ambassador in Moscow, that if any Allied aircraft were sent to drop arms on Warsaw they would not be permitted to land on Soviet-occupied territory. Realizing that the Red Army was not coming to the aid of the Poles, Hitler halted the German withdrawal from Warsaw and ordered the total destruction of the city and the slaughter of its entire population of men, women and children.

Ward was promoted to the rank of lieutenant in the Armia Krajowa and awarded the Cross of Valour by the AK's supreme Commander, General Bor Komorowski. When not busy sending plaintive radio messages to London, Ward was embroiled in street fighting against the Germans. He sustained a leg wound at a time when qualified doctors were scarce and medical students were performing emergency surgery. For the second time he was awarded the Polish Cross of Valour.

In her Warsaw apartment, Maria Jarnuszkiewicz, an AK cryptographer, sat huddled over an illegal radio set and decoded messages from London by the dim light of a candle. She was dismayed to read that the British government had rejected the AK's requests for substantial help. The uprising was doomed. Suddenly a shot rang out and a bullet pierced the heavy curtains and lodged in the window frame. Her young brother had foolishly started to clean an illegally-obtained pistol, while it was loaded. Maria extinguished the candle and hoped that nobody had heard the shot above the sound of distant gunfire. The next day she carefully hid the decoded messages under some items in her shopping bag and walked through the streets to deliver the bad news to the AK's high command. She knew that if the Germans discovered the secret messages, she and her relatives would be tortured and then shot. The same fate was certain if the Germans searched her apartment and discovered her forbidden radio and typewriter. Although Maria was deciphering London's replies to Ward's messages she did not know him personally. I learned that members of the AK had adopted pseudonyms and I realized that only a few people would have been aware of Ward's true identity. As I seemed to have reached a dead end in Poland, I thought perhaps I might locate him or discover more information about him in England. I could not ask the Polish communist government to assist me. I was supposed to be visiting countries behind the Iron Curtain for purely business reasons. The communist authorities did not tolerate the presence of western researchers and journalists during the Cold War.

When the Polish winter weather became severe, I stopped travelling by car and booked my next visit to Warsaw on a German Lufthansa flight, via Frankfurt. Shortly before take-off the pilot greeted the passengers over the public address system and announced, 'Your stewardesses in first class this morning are Ursula (someone) and Baroness (something) von Richthofen.' A stewardess weighing about eight stone sat down in the vacant seat next to me and said,

'We have to sit down to ensure equal distribution of the weight.' I conceitedly assumed that the truth was that she fancied me. 'Are you Ursula, or von Richthofen?' I enquired. She was von Richthofen. 'I knew your dad, the Red Baron,' I joked. She smiled at me, 'Did you really? He was actually my uncle.' I said, 'I did not know him personally. I am not so old, but I know all about him because I was also an airman.'

When I mentioned that I had served on a B-24 Liberator squadron, she told me, 'The captain of this plane was in the Luftwaffe and he flew Liberators too. I will tell him that you are on board and I am sure he will like to meet you.' I thought the young woman surely was mistaken. Liberators were American planes. Perhaps the pilot was pulling her leg. Halfway to Frankfurt, she reappeared and said, 'The captain requests you to join him in the cockpit for a cup of coffee, if you would be so kind.' I sat in the jump seat and we chatted about my time on an RAF bomber squadron and the German pilot's time in the Luftwaffe. I said, 'The stewardess thinks that you flew American Liberator bombers during the war.' He replied:

> Yes, that is true. The Americans crashed and force-landed many planes in the desert during the North Africa campaign. Some of the Liberators were out of fuel, but there was not much wrong with them, so our mechanics repaired the best of them by cannibalizing others. We put our insignia on them and used them as transport planes. I liked flying the Liberators.

On hearing this, I thought it was fortunate that the Germans did not leave the American markings on the planes and bomb our Royal Air Force bases with them! Many years later I mentioned the German Liberator pilot to my friend Freddie Rosier (later Air Chief Marshal Sir Frederick). Freddie had been on patrol over the desert when he saw, from the cockpit of his Spitfire, an abandoned German Stuka dive-bomber. Back at base, he took some cans of fuel and drove out into the desert with a mechanic in a 'borrowed' jeep. They found the Stuka was not badly damaged. After they had refuelled it and the mechanic had tinkered with the engine, Freddie flew it back to his base. 'I had a lot of fun flying it,' he told me. As an eighteen-year-old pupil pilot at the time of the desert campaign, I would have loved to fly a Stuka. It looked like a lot more fun than flying a heavy bomber.

After my chance meeting with the German Lufthansa pilot I decided to seek out more war veterans during future business trips to Germany. Meanwhile, I was still busily trying to trace the elusive Ward.

I contacted the occupiers of the house where Ward's parents had lived during the war. The parents had died and the house had changed hands a couple of times since then. I thought that surely someone in Birmingham would know of a local war hero like Ward, but there was no record of him there. Eventually, I traced his uncle, who told me that Ward returned to England after the war and then disappeared.

The family never saw him again. His mother had thought that he worked for either the War Office or Foreign Office. He could only be contacted through a solicitor and it was rumoured that he lived on an ocean-going yacht for a while. He seemed to have disappeared off the face of the earth, but I was determined to continue my search, so I painstakingly waded through reams of records held by various official bodies. I discovered that, at the end of 1944, arrangements were made for Ward to be picked up by plane from Sulejow, situated off the Radom road near Piotrkow, south of Warsaw. A message, dated 11 November, from a Lieutenant Colonel Wigginton to Lieutenant Colonel Threlfall, informed him, 'One of the people to be picked up is a political personage of the highest importance. Another is a high officer in the Armia Krajowa, who recently went to Poland, and the third is an RAF officer named Ward.' It seems, however, that Ward did not return to England by air. For some mysterious reason, he received instructions to report to the Russian authorities, and he eventually departed to England from the Soviet port of Odessa in March 1945. I was unable to discover what he had been doing during his final six months abroad.

After his return to England, he was promoted to the rank of flight lieutenant and awarded the Military Cross. He left the air force in 1949. My guess is that the British so-called 'intelligence' services recruited him and he probably embarked on another series of clandestine activities. My interest in Ward stemmed from the fact that we had both been involved in the 1944 Warsaw Uprising, albeit in vastly different capacities. As it seemed that he no longer existed, I wonder if his luck finally ran out during the Cold War after he had survived so many dangerous exploits in the Second World War. I was disappointed that I failed to find him. Many years later, I discovered that the Polish Underground Movement Study Trust in London had also tried in vain to trace him.

CHAPTER THREE

During the Second World War, I was listening to the radio at the start of the six o'clock news. I expected the newsreader to announce that German planes had dropped bombs at random. The public was not allowed to know which British towns were bombed and we joked that random had been bombed so often it must be totally destroyed by now. To my surprise, a voice announced between the chimes of Big Ben, 'Tolling the death knell of old England.' Oblivious of the interruption, the BBC newsreader proceeded to give details of last night's attacks by the RAF on German targets. At that point, the voice asked, 'How many churches did they destroy?' Similar comments continued throughout the news. The listeners learned later that the interruptions were made by a German radio station broadcasting cleverly on the BBC's wavelength. The voice was that of William Joyce who was dubbed 'Lord Haw-Haw' by his British listeners because of his phoney upper-class nasal drawl when he began his propaganda broadcasts with 'Jarmany calling – Jarmany calling'. For the next few days, the British newsreaders attempted a rapid gabble through the news, scarcely pausing for breath. Every brief interval was filled with martial music to ensure that the German station could not intrude. Eventually, the Germans stopped interrupting the BBC news and Joyce started regularly broadcasting German propaganda interspersed with details of British prisoners of war. The British government announced that people listening to the German broadcasts were 'assisting the enemy'. I failed to see what harm was done by worried parents who hoped to hear from the Germans that their missing aircrew sons were not dead. They were supposed to endure the agony of a long wait until news from the International Red Cross came through official channels. While William Joyce was broadcasting to Britain, a British journalist named Sefton Delmer was making British propaganda broadcasts in the German language to Germany. He pretended that he was speaking from a German radio station.

William Joyce was an Irish/American who had emigrated to Germany before the war, but retained his British passport. He was hanged for treason in London in 1946. I cannot remember how Sefton Delmer spent his post-war years, but he certainly would not have survived for long if we had lost the war.

During the last days of the war, Joyce had made final propaganda broadcasts from Germany in which he predicted that the western Allies would soon need Germany's help to combat a threat from the Soviet Union. Sure enough, it was not long before the Cold War started. Churchill declared that an 'Iron Curtain has descended across the European Continent', isolating our gallant wartime friends under brutal Stalinist dictatorships. The western Allies began to re-organize and re-arm the defeated German forces[1] and Britain started a frantic re-armament campaign.

I thought there was either going to be a real war with the Soviet Union very soon or there would eventually be opportunities for trade with the underdeveloped countries of the eastern bloc. At any event, it was time to add Russian to my other languages. My tutor, Bedrich, was a typical Austrian Jewish intellectual. He spoke Russian and all other Slav languages. Under his guidance I studied all the great Russian authors such as Tolstoy, Dostoyevsky, Gogol and Turgenyev. During the immediate post-war years, new books were unobtainable, so I searched the bookshops of London districts such as Hampstead for second-hand books to aid my studies. On one occasion, a bookseller offered me the collected works of Lenin at a bargain price and he was surprised when I declined his offer but, at that time, I knew little and cared even less about communism.

It took me about six months to completely master the reading and writing of the Russian alphabet, and then the language itself presented no problem and I rapidly became fluent. I kept plain covers on my books when travelling on public transport in case nosey fellow passengers, being aware of the Cold War threat, should regard me as a spy. The Americans began to purge their citizens in a frenzy of what later became known as McCarthyism and anti-communist hysteria spread across the Atlantic. Bedrich, fearing that I might acquire his Austrian accent, advised me to find a native Russian teacher. By chance I found Sue Cherny, a Russian émigré who coached me in her spare time. Her father, a banker, had fled penniless from Russia during the October revolution. Shortly after arriving in England, Sue responded to a newspaper advertisement for a 'Cook General'. She understood that generals were of high rank, so she was surprised to find that she was to be quite an ordinary cook, not a senior officer. From her, I acquired an excellent Russian accent.

Between them the Poles and Czechoslovaks had contributed over twenty-five fighter and bomber squadrons to the wartime Royal Air Force. I wondered what had happened to the thousands of airmen who returned home to their families after the war and lived under the puppet communist governments foisted on them by Stalin. My British colleagues and I had flown together with a Polish squadron in 1944, and I wondered what the Polish airmen now thought of the western Allies who had so shamefully betrayed them while attempting to appease the murderous Stalin. The British and United States governments agreed, while the war was still raging, that Stalin could retain control of the illegally occupied eastern half of Poland. Consequently, thousands of Poles serving alongside our forces faced the choice of either returning home after the war to live under the heel of their arch-enemies or seeking refuge as lifelong exiles in any western countries that would accept them. I was mainly interested in the men who returned home and I wanted to find some of them.

My friend Jozef Polilejko suffered at the hands of the communists before the Soviet Union entered the war. Deaf to his father's entreaties to stay and work on the family farm, Jozef joined the Polish Air Force. While Hitler ranted about the German need for 'Lebensraum' and war seemed inevitable, the twenty-year-old Jozef qualified as a bomber pilot. The small Polish Air Force had more pilots than planes when, on 1 September 1939, Hitler launched a savage attack on the ill-equipped Polish forces.

Despite valiant, but short-lived, Polish resistance, the powerful German Army swiftly overran the western half of the country while the Red Army illegally occupied the eastern half. When the two invaders met they held a joint victory celebration. As their enemies approached some Polish pilots attempted to evacuate their few remaining aircraft to safety in nearby neutral countries. Desperately short of fuel, Jozef made an emergency landing in neutral Latvia hoping to refuel there, but to his dismay he was promptly arrested and his plane was impounded.

Incarcerated in a concentration camp near Riga, Jozef and fellow air force prisoners were hastily digging an escape tunnel when disaster struck again. Russian forces invaded Latvia and transported the Polish airmen to a camp near Moscow. Conditions in the Latvian camp had been tolerable, but now the airmen experienced harsh treatment at the hands of the Russians. Although Poland was not officially at war with Russia, Jozef and his companions were subjected to hours of interrogation, brutality and threats. All the Polish air force officers were segregated and destined to be massacred with others at a place named Katyn. When Jozef was instructed to join the officers he pointed out that he was not an officer; he was a corporal. The Russians had assumed that all pilots were officers and they accused Jozef of lying to save his skin. Brutal interrogation followed as the Russians attempted to break his defiant spirit, but eventually Jozef convinced his tormenters that he was not lying about his rank. He avoided the fate of over 4,500 officers who, on Stalin's orders, were slaughtered at Katyn in 1940 with their hands bound behind their backs.

After the interrogations had been concluded, Jozef and other airmen were crammed into cattle trucks for a gruelling journey from Moscow to Murmansk. As the prison train had low priority on the railway network, it was frequently delayed and the journey to Murmansk took three weeks. Now and again the Russian guards threw a few salt herrings to the hungry prisoners in the cattle trucks. The prisoners' only opportunity to drink was when the train stopped to refuel and the guards allowed them to gulp stale water out of the fire buckets on the stations. Upon arrival at Murmansk, Jozef and about 150 other men were locked in the filthy hold of a coal steamer bound for a desolate area north of Archangel. When the ship neared its destination, violent storms prevented it from discharging its cargo and it remained at sea for a further five days. All this time, the prisoners remained crammed together in the dark and stinking dampness of the locked hold. When half of the men died of cold and starvation, Jozef found himself lying on the ice-cold corpses of men from his old squadron. When the surviving prisoners eventually disembarked, the guards set them to work unloading material that was to be used for the construction of an airfield. As the starving men unloaded cartons of axle grease and passed them from hand to hand they each took a mouthful and every carton was nearly empty when it reached the last man. Construction of the airfield started and the starving airmen, working as slave labourers, desperately searched in vain for dogs to eat.

Jozef realized that hard work in the Arctic climate was killing him. He feared that he would not survive through another harsh winter of deprivation, but then it seemed that a miracle occurred. In 1941 German troops pushed eastwards and invaded Russia. In due course Britain formed an alliance with the Soviet Union and made an agreement for the release of the innocent Polish prisoners. Jozef and his starving colleagues were transported in passenger trains to Archangel where they were accommodated in hotels while Royal Air Force uniforms were issued to them and, most importantly, they received proper food. Within a matter of days they boarded a British ship bound for Scotland and, despite attacks by German planes, they arrived safely at their destination. Jozef noticed that several well-known Polish politicians, travelling under assumed names, accompanied the airmen. A Russian Army captain joined the Polish group and pleaded for help to disguise himself as a Pole. He claimed that his knowledge of the Russians' atrocities against the Polish prisoners made him liable to arrest by his authorities. He said they would kill him because he simply knew too much.

Shortly after arriving in England the Polish pilots were incorporated into the Royal Air Force, treated like raw recruits and sent to elementary flying schools for training on Tiger Moths. The impatient Poles were keen to get into action against the enemy immediately, but they were told, 'You must first learn English.'

Jozef and his friends protested, 'We want to shoot at the Germans, not talk at them. Let's get on with the war!' Despite their protestations, they were forced to study English and, although they were already qualified pilots, were put through the Royal Air Force's flying training schools as though they had never been off the ground.

Although constantly dogged by ill health, Jozef managed to gain his Royal Air Force flying badge. He then joined the famous Number 303 (Polish) Spitfire Squadron. The squadron's claim to fame was that its score of planes shot down in the Battle of Britain was greater than that of any other unit of the Royal Air Force or of the Luftwaffe.

In August 1944 Jozef was chasing V1 flying bombs en route to London. At the same time my Liberator squadron was bombing in support of the south of France invasion until ordered to take on the unaccustomed task of dropping parachute containers of arms to the Armia Krajowa in the besieged Polish capital. We both wished our respective roles had been reversed. After the war Jozef was loath to talk about his dreadful experiences at the hands of the Russians. Twelve years after we first met he mentioned that he had been a prisoner. Two years later, after much gentle persuasion, he began to disclose details of his ordeals to me. In conversations he often reflected that, if Hitler had not attacked the Soviet Union, he and his fellow airmen would certainly have died of cold and starvation in 1941. 'That swine Hitler actually saved my life,' he told me. The airfields constructed by Jozef and his fellow slave workers were used later by British and Russian airmen flying some of the 3,000 fighter planes that Britain supplied to our new ally, the villainous Stalin.

Many other people suffered at the hands of Stalin before the start of the Second World War. My friend Jim Inward was serving as an engineer in the Royal Air Force when the Russians attacked Finland. There was great sympathy in Britain for the unfortunate Finns and I remember hearing their Prime Minister's appeal for help on our radio. The Finnish Air Force obtained some British Gloster Gladiator biplanes and the RAF sent Jim to work on them in Finland, in the guise of a civilian worker. During Finland's unsuccessful Winter Campaign he taught engineers to maintain the Gladiators. When Finland eventually capitulated, he avoided capture by illegally escaping across the frontier into Sweden. The Swedish authorities arrested him on a false charge of sabotage and flung him into gaol. By the time he eventually returned to England and resumed his Royal Air Force career, he had developed such an aversion to certain items of the Swedish prison diet of root vegetables that he could not tolerate them for the rest of his life. During the Second World War he re-mustered to aircrew and won the Distinguished Flying Cross.

When Hitler attacked Russia in 1941, the Finns' hatred of the Russians led them to ally themselves with the Germans. Automatically, this made them enemies of the western Allies but the British people never regarded them as such. After the war the government of Finland awarded their Winter Campaign Medal to Jim but, although he was no longer in the Royal Air Force, the British authorities ruled that he must not wear it in Britain. The same authorities tried to impose similar restrictions on veterans who received war medals from other foreign governments. Some veterans ignored the ban and truculently wore their outlawed foreign medals openly. Presumably the authorities did not impose restrictions on our fellow war veteran, the Duke of Edinburgh, a wartime junior naval officer, who regularly wears a most impressive display of foreign decorations on his various splendid uniforms.

Not all veterans of the Second World War are willing to talk or write about the dreadful ordeals they endured at the hands of the Germans and Russians. My friend Tomiczek served as a B-24 Liberator pilot of 1586 Flight (later 301 Polish Squadron) of the Royal Air Force. Like me he was engaged on support of resistance groups behind enemy lines and we both flew to Warsaw from Brindisi during the 1944 Uprising. Just like my friend Jozef, he had suffered imprisonment by the Russians, but he never talked about his ordeals. Of course, he had to be careful while his country was still under Communist Russian domination and afterwards it seemed that nobody cared about what happened to him in the past. When we first met at his home in Poland and shook hands, I asked him, 'What caused those hard lumps in the palms of your hands?'

He told me that in 1939 the Russians had condemned him to hard labour in a stone quarry. Handling huge lumps of rock every day over a long period had caused permanent damage to his hands. I was surprised that he later managed to manipulate the controls of an aeroplane despite his injuries. Tomiczek kindly acted as my guide during a visit to Lamsdorf, a First and Second World War prison camp. The Germans sent soldiers of the Armia Krajowa there after the collapse of the 1944 Warsaw Uprising and, as there was no proper accommodation for them, they lived outside in trenches.

Publisher's note:
1 But not officially until 1956.

CHAPTER FOUR

During one of my business trips to Warsaw the state television service interviewed me for an official film about the 1944 Uprising. Another Polish friend, Gosczynski, attended with me to assist with interpreting and, although he had carried out more flights during the Warsaw Uprising than I had, he made no mention of his own experiences. Life under the Stalinist dictatorships behind the Iron Curtain had taught people to maintain a low profile and never disclose personal information to anyone.

After completing the day's business engagements, I decided to get some fresh air. I gingerly stepped out of my hotel onto the icy pavement. Apart from one or two official cars, the streets of Warsaw were totally devoid of motor traffic. With bells clanging, the occasional trams rattled and scrunched their way along the snow-covered streets. People hunched their shoulders against the bitter wind as they skirted round the piles of snow on the pavements and glanced hopefully at the empty shop windows. Here and there, people queued patiently outside sparsely-stocked food stores. Many people wore homemade fur hats fashioned from rabbit or dog skin. Ordinary shoes were not suitable for use in the foul Polish climate, so I was wearing the short cowboy boots that I had bought during a recent business trip to Mexico. I paused to look at a display of illustrations in the dingy windows of the Official Press Office. The theme was the 1944 Warsaw Uprising. The fierce cold was penetrating the legs of my trousers, so I decided to go into the office to thaw out. An officious woman approached and I tried to talk to her in Polish. The hostile expression on her face spoke volumes when I inadvertently used a couple of Russian words, so I switched to German. She indicated with hand gestures that I should sit down and then hurried away. Had she gone to phone the police? I anxiously checked that I had my passport in my pocket and waited uneasily. After what seemed like an eternity, an elderly man appeared and greeted me in German with a strong Polish accent. I explained that I had noticed the window display of illustrations relating to the 1944 Warsaw Uprising. When I mentioned that I had flown to Poland with parachute containers of supplies for the Armia Krajowa he shook my hand and embraced me. Tears came to his eyes as he told me that he was a veteran of the Armia Krajowa and he had fought in Warsaw during the uprising. If I wanted photographs and information about the Armia Krajowa, he would arrange a meeting with his friend, Colonel Wojciech Borzobohaty VM.

Colonel Borzobohaty was a career officer of the pre-war Polish Army who, with others, had been involved in the formation of the Armia Krajowa out of a variety of individual resistance groups in the early days of the Second World War. Although repeatedly wounded by the Germans, he never surrendered. He was commanding an Armia Krajowa group in the large Radom/Kiece area when General Bor, the AK Supreme Commander, called on him to bring his soldiers to the aid of the insurgents in Warsaw. On their way to Warsaw, his troops encountered fierce Russian as well as German opposition. He told me:

> We had run out of ammunition for our PIAT gun and our situation looked hopeless until, in the middle of the night, a British plane dropped a load of parachute containers. We opened the containers and found a consignment of PIAT shells. It seemed like a miracle. We blessed the brave boys of the RAF and prayed that they would return safely to their far away base.

While resisting arrest by the communists one month after the end of the war, Borzobohaty was shot four times by the UB (Communist Security Police). Together with other senior officers of the Armia Krajowa, he was flung into the infamous Xth Pavilion Gaol on Warsaw's Rakowiecka Street. Following six months of interrogation and torture, he was charged with attempting to subvert the communist system and, after a mock trial behind the closed doors of his prison cell, a military tribunal sentenced him to death. After considerable delay and legal wrangling, the sentence was commuted to ten years' imprisonment. An amnesty in 1947 reduced his sentence to five years but, when he was due for release from prison, he faced further interrogations and trumped-up charges. This time he was accused of espionage, collaboration with the German Gestapo and military action against the state. His release was cancelled and he endured a further three years of solitary confinement and torture. When he eventually left prison he was a physical wreck. He was deprived of civil rights for another ten years and restricted to menial work. Many years after his release from prison, his frail elderly figure was to be seen each day waiting for a tram to take him to a café where he filled his little mess tin with food for his bedridden invalid wife who had also served in the Armia Krajowa. He told me, 'One day on the tram, I saw a man who had tortured me in prison. He recognized me and jumped off the tram.' I asked, 'Didn't you follow him?' He replied, 'I could not do that. The tram was going so fast it was a wonder he did not kill himself when he jumped off.' If I had been Borzobohaty, I would not have rested until I had found that man again and pushed him under a tram. When I said that, Borzobohaty looked aghast and said, 'It is better to try to forget the past and make the best of life as it is now.' We remained firm friends until his death.

Towards the end of his life, he scraped together enough money for an exit visa, allowing him to travel to Paris for operations on his eyes. The ophthalmic surgeon asked him, 'What are all those marks on your body?' When he explained that they were the result of repeated torture by the communists, the French surgeon said, 'I will not charge you anything for this operation.' Borzobohaty chose Paris for his operations because he had relatives there. His grandfather and three uncles had participated in the January uprising of 1863 and the Czar's court sentenced them all to banishment in Siberia. However, the oldest of them, a commander in the Nowogrodek district, escaped to France. He was sentenced to death in absentia, but he survived and raised a family in Paris. In 1983 Borzobohaty was permitted by the communist authorities to publish a book about the Armia Krajowa entitled *Jodla* (pronounced Yodwa). He was only allowed access to a limited amount of paper, so circulation of the book was severely restricted.

I am the proud owner of a signed and dedicated copy but, sadly, my poor command of the Polish language prevents me from understanding much of it. My friendship with Borzobohaty opened many doors for me and when the Polish government eventually permitted the formation of the Armia Krajowa Association in Warsaw, Borzobohaty became its first president. At the Association's inaugural ceremony I was elected to honorary membership.

By the time of Borzobohaty's death, the Solidarity-led government was in power and the recently-elected President Lech Walesa promoted him posthumously and invested him with a high award. During the whole of his military career he had repeatedly declined promotion saying, 'Just take care of my soldiers – not me!' The arrest and sham trial of Borzobohaty during the post-war Stalinist tyranny had been organized by the fanatical communist military prosecutor Helena Wolinska, who was responsible for the execution of numerous prominent Polish anti-Nazi resistance patriots. Wolinska left Poland for Great Britain in 1968. Following the fall of Communism in 1989, the newly-elected Polish authorities repeatedly demanded her extradition to be tried for Stalinist crimes, but the British Home Office refused to extradite her on the grounds that she might be unjustly persecuted by the Poles. The misguided decision of the Home Office ensured that the tyrannical Wolinska could remain safely in Britain until her demise in 2007.

The much persecuted Wojciech Borzobohaty, one of Wolinska's many innocent victims and a true Polish patriot, was an exceptionally kind man with a quiet unassuming manner. He was also one of the bravest men I have ever met and I value greatly my memories of our years of close personal friendship.

CHAPTER FIVE

During my first business trips behind the Iron Curtain I had been surprised to find that my most prevalent and active competitors were German manufacturers. The governments of the countries that had been overrun by the Germans during the war showed no post-war commercial prejudice against their former enemies. On the basis that 'business is business', they were willing to trade with the Germans if it was in their national interest to do so. I was also trading with West German firms that had rapidly rebuilt their ruined engineering factories and modernized their products. I spent a good deal of time in West Berlin and was amazed how quickly the population had recovered from the terrible wartime devastation. The Berliners were so resilient that they had withstood continual air bombardment and even the devastating Russian assault on their city. The vengeful Red Army was forced to suffer enormous casualties in 1945 as it fought through the streets of Berlin against German soldiers and armed civilians who were not ready to give up the fight despite the hopelessness of their situation. The planners of our mighty strategic bomber offensive had been clearly unaware of the stoical nature of the Berliners. The main purpose of the Allies' bombing raids on Berlin had been to sap the morale of the inhabitants but clearly it failed and, sadly, the lives of a great many Allied airmen were lost in the vain attempt. It would have been far more sensible to concentrate on bombing oil refineries. After all, a shortage of fuel, not a reduction in morale, eventually brought German aircraft and tanks to a stop. Although the intensive bombing of Berlin was largely a waste of our airmen, aircraft and bombs, perhaps it had some value as an extravagant way of mollifying the ever-critical Stalin.

In the early 1950s one of my suppliers, a West Berlin firm named Werner, opened a subsidiary factory at Geisenheim on the banks of the Rhein. The staff members were typical beer-swilling Berliners who drank the local Rhein wine in huge quantities. During a visit to their factory, the directors invited me to join them for an evening pub crawl of the local wine bars. Towards the end of the evening they said they wanted to take me to an especially interesting bar. As we entered I noticed some pictures of German planes on the walls. The bar owner had only one arm and my companions informed me, 'He was a Luftwaffe pilot.' They then told him, 'This is our friend Mr Auton from England. He flew bombers in the Royal Air Force.' I assumed that we had shot the man's arm off and I was not sure how to react. In the dim light of the bar I looked at one of the pictures on the wall and asked, 'Is that a Heinkel?' He looked disparagingly at me and growled, 'No, it is a Junkers 88.' His facial expression seemed to add the word *Dummkopf*. I then foolishly said that we never saw much of the German air force. (What I really meant was that aircraft recognition is not easy in the dark.) As he turned away with a look of displeasure on his face, I saw that he was supporting himself on a crutch. No doubt I would have been capable of a more sensible conversation with him if I had not been quite so befuddled by an excess of the local wine.

During the early post-war years, the Germans had no government of their own. A civilian body called the Allied Control Commission administered the country. One evening I was with some of my German business acquaintances in a wine bar in the Drosselgasse at Ruedesheim. The locals were in high spirits as Rhinelanders always are in the wine bars – singing and dancing as though they had not a care in the world. I noticed three American men and a woman of the Control Commission quietly drinking and looking rather out of place in the boisterous atmosphere of the wine bar. The men were talking earnestly together and ignoring their bored-looking female colleague. I decided to pretend to be a German and play a joke on them. Approaching their table, I made a slight bow in customary German fashion and said to the men, '*Gestatten sie bitte*' (permit me) and to the woman, '*Darf Ich bitten?*' The men looked startled and one said to the woman, 'I guess he wants to dance with you.' The young woman's expression of utter boredom was replaced by a charming smile as I led her onto the crowded dance floor. While we danced I talked to her in German and discovered that she hardly knew more than a dozen words. Valiantly trying to understand me, she said, 'Ich bin Americanerin – aus New York.' I held her close and, adopting a phoney German accent, uttered in guttural English, 'Okay, Yankee-doodle,' followed by a few saucy and flirtatious remarks in a mixture of German and broken English. When the music stopped, I led her back to her colleagues and performed the appropriate German hand-kissing ritual. She was a trifle flushed as I left her and returned to my own table. I imagined her telling her colleagues what a charming German I was. I thought she might want to kill me if she found out that I was just an English hoaxer, so I suggested to my German companions that we move on to a different wine bar.

Few places on earth were as depressing as Prague on a damp October afternoon at the height of the Cold War. On the pretext of market research, I made my first visit to the Czechoslovak capital in early 1950. I was hoping to find out what had happened to men who returned home at the end of the war after serving in five Czechoslovak squadrons of the Royal Air Force. I made appointments to visit the State Trading Corporations on the day after my arrival, so I had the first day free for sightseeing. I took my furled umbrella and set off to look at architecturally magnificent buildings that, in those days, were as black as coal. Apart from clanging trams, there was no traffic on the streets. A few shabbily-dressed pedestrians with hangdog expressions wandered along the pavements. I doubted that the poverty-stricken government of Czechoslovakia would be able to purchase goods from the west, but my only way to visit Prague was with the aid of a business visa. I was looking into a sparsely-stocked shop window when a man on the other side of the street shouted at me, 'Hallo Shamberline – Shamberline!' I quickly realized that he was taunting me with the name of our former prime minister, Neville Chamberlain, whose pathetic attempts to negotiate with Hitler had preceded the German occupation of Czechoslovakia. Newspaper cartoonists of the time had always depicted Chamberlain with a furled umbrella. I decided never again to carry one in Czechoslovakia.

In 1938, when the German invasion of their country was

imminent, hundreds of Czech pilots had fled to Poland and joined the Polish air force. Upon the fall of Poland, they escaped to France and joined the French forces. Once again, they had to flee when France fell and this time they came to Britain – the only country still opposing the Nazi menace. At that time our country stood alone in the face of the overwhelming might of the German Wehrmacht that was poised to cross the narrow English Channel. Britain was the Czechs' last refuge. If Britain fell, their final destination would be a Nazi concentration camp. The Royal Air Force formed the Czech pilots into four fighter squadrons and one bomber squadron. A Czech told me, 'We are grateful to Britain for giving us the opportunity to continue the fight for Czechoslovak freedom.' Little did he realize that so many of his compatriots would not survive long enough to see his country finally free of tyranny. Due to wartime official secrecy, the British people knew nothing about the arrival of the Czechoslovak airmen. I first became aware of them when I saw men in strange dark-blue uniforms on Peterborough railway station. Being inquisitive, I stood near them and tried to guess what language they were speaking. It was unintelligible Czech and I later discovered that they were wearing French uniforms.

After much probing during my business visits to Czechoslovakia, I learned that the country was temporarily a free democracy at the end of the war. The returning airmen were feted as heroes when they marched through the streets of Prague in RAF uniforms, but in 1948 the communists took power; the country became a Soviet satellite state and the men who had fought against the Germans alongside our own men were cruelly persecuted by their new masters.

Former Flight Lieutenant Altman AFC, a Czech pilot since 1929, had escaped to England with his wife and eight-year-old daughter Jarmila in May 1939. During a very distinguished wartime career in the Royal Air Force, he served on Number 24 Squadron. The family lived at 29 West Avenue in Hendon and Jarmila attended school in Maidenhead. Altman's logbook shows that the aircraft he flew included Electras, Stinsons, Flamingos, Fokker XIIs, Dominies, Dakotas, Hudsons, Oxfords and Wellingtons. His passengers included Winston Churchill, Anthony Eden, Clement Attlee, Stafford Cripps, Sir Archibald Sinclair, the Duke of Gloucester, Lord Mountbatten, Lord Trenchard, Prince Olaf of Norway and a host of other very important people. He returned to Prague in 1945 and, the following year, joined CSA, the Czechoslovak civil airline.

Disaster struck his family when the communists took power in 1948. After being sacked from his job with CSA, he decided to return to England and accept the offer of a job with a private airline. He obtained visas and airline tickets for his family, but he was immediately arrested, beaten up, charged with treason and flung into prison. His only 'crime' was that he had lived in capitalist Britain and served in the Royal Air Force. Following a mock trial, he received a death sentence that was later commuted to twelve years' slave labour in the uranium ore mines where he contracted a life-threatening disease. After eight years he was released to work as a manual labourer on building sites. He lost all civil rights and was restricted to poorly paid, menial work for the remainder of his life. The communist authorities also persecuted all the members of his family. They were evicted from the luxury accommodation that had been presented to them by the previous grateful government and, for many years, seven of them had to exist in only two rooms. When her father was arrested, Jarmila found that the police had taken away not only her father's documents, but also her schoolbooks, so she went to the police headquarters and pleaded for the return of her property. She succeeded in retrieving her schoolbooks and, unnoticed by the police, she also obtained her father's precious flying logbook.

After years of communist persecution, poverty and ill health, Frantisek Altman AFC died when struck by a vehicle in a Prague street. He was just one of hundreds of Royal Air Force volunteers who suffered persecution at the hands of communist regimes during the years of Stalinist tyranny. Some men were shot or beaten to death while allegedly resisting arrest or attempting to escape. I was surreptitiously seeking to uncover their harrowing stories during my business trips behind the Iron Curtain.

Among those trapped behind the Iron Curtain, I discovered a number of British widows of Czechoslovaks who had served in

Britain. Ailsa Domanova was one of those women. While working as a young Red Cross nurse in wartime London she had married the Assistant Czechoslovak Defence Attaché. Ailsa's husband served with distinction as a military parachutist in some of the war's most dangerous battles and when the war ended he returned home to a hero's welcome, with his young British bride. When the communists took power in 1948, Ailsa's husband was arrested and imprisoned because he had served in wartime Britain. In mid-winter she and her baby, together with the contents of her home, were thrown out into the snow. She was destitute and, in desperation, turned to the British Embassy for help. At the embassy she explained her predicament and asked for a loan for food. She was told that in order to get twenty pounds she must first produce a written guarantee from her mother in England that the loan would be repaid. In the meantime it seems that she and the baby could starve for all they cared.

Another British war bride in similar difficulties was told by an official at the Embassy that she should not have married a foreigner. Obviously, she was no longer regarded as British. I wonder if any distressed British war brides of Americans may have encountered similar treatment by our embassy officials in the USA.

Czech Sergeant Siska's RAF Wellington bomber crashed into the ice-cold waters of the North Sea in mid-winter and the crew had to endure five days in an open rubber dinghy. They soon began to suffer the effects of hypothermia and had nothing to eat or drink. One by one the men died and the survivors became too weak to push the corpses out of the dinghy. When they noticed mines bobbing around them they knew that nobody would come to rescue them. When only Siska and his navigator remained alive, they attempted unsuccessfully to end their suffering by drinking seawater mixed with morphine from the first aid kit. Semi-conscious, they were eventually washed up on the Dutch coast where, in their bedraggled state, they were thought to be Germans. When, during interrogation, they were discovered to be Czech members of the Royal Air Force, their German captors told them that they were traitors who should have joined the Luftwaffe. Siska's feet were severely frostbitten and the German doctors told him that they would both be amputated. He protested against amputation and was sent to a prison camp with his damaged feet untreated.

When a Swiss representative of the International Red Cross visited the camp, he told the Germans that, in view of Siska's severe injuries, he should be sent back to England. After forcing him to walk painfully back and forth on the bare wooden floor the Germans declared, 'There's nothing wrong with him – we have seen him playing football'. They were determined to keep him in captivity. One day he saw a guard hitting an English prisoner with the butt of a rifle. The prisoner soundly berated the guard and cited the Geneva Convention. Siska told me:

> I decided to follow the example of the most truculent British prisoners and make myself a nuisance to the guards. In fact, I became even more antagonistic than the British were. As punishment for my disruptive behaviour, I was eventually sent to Colditz where I remained until the American Army arrived and liberated the place.

Mike Scott, a member of my technical staff, had also been transferred to Colditz Castle after he had escaped four times from other prison camps. On his first business trip to Poland with me, we were passing Poznan railway station when he said, 'I recognize this place. I have been here before.' I said, 'You told me that you had never been in Poland.' Mike explained:

> I was brought here in a closed truck when I was a prisoner of war. The place was seething with German troops and there were signs in German everywhere, so I thought I was in Germany. As soon as I arrived here, I was taken under armed guard to a nearby prison camp, so I did not see anything except the railway station.

I asked him, 'How far away was the prison camp?' He replied, 'It was a long time ago. I cannot remember exactly. It was not far and it seemed like an old Napoleonic fort.' I said, 'If it was an old fort, it probably still exists. If you want to go and see it again, I will ask my Polish friends, Bogdan and Barbara, to take you there.' Mike had been a junior British Army officer when the Germans captured him at the time of the retreat to Dunkirk and he spent the rest of the war in prison camps. He escaped four times, only to be recaptured each time after only a short spell of freedom. I asked him, 'Why were you so frequently selected to be one of the escapers?' He told me, 'As a pre-war mining engineer and tunnelling expert, I was a member of the escape committees.' Although Mike succeeded in enraging the Germans by escaping so frequently, his ingenuity and expertise failed him as soon as he was on the outside. I often chided him over his failure to remain at liberty. 'You could not get far without speaking German,' I told him, 'You should have learned German from the Dutch, Belgian and Polish prisoners and practised by talking to the guards.' He said, 'The guards? We did not want to have any contact with those goons. We didn't like them.' I urged him to tell me about the guards. He said, 'Some of the older ones were alright. They took photographs and gave us pictures of ourselves in exchange for chocolate and cigarettes from our Red Cross parcels.' I said, 'I am sure they would not have objected to you speaking in German to them and you could have become proficient in a few months. If I had been there with you, we would have got back home after our first escape.' I wanted to know what mistakes had led to his recapture, so I urged him to tell me what he did after each escape. He said:

One time, I was hiding in a railway tunnel, eating some of the chocolate that I had hoarded for six months ready for the escape. Suddenly, some Hitler Youth lads in uniform appeared and marched me off to the local police station at gunpoint. That was the end of that attempt. I was kept in the police cells overnight and during the evening, two of the boys who had captured me turned up at the police station and demanded some of my chocolate. Another time, I was walking through a forest when I encountered a man who looked like a gamekeeper. He was with a young girl and he sent her to fetch some soldiers while he kept me covered with his shotgun, and then I was back inside once again.

After his fourth escape, the Germans punished him by packing him off to the supposedly escape-proof Colditz Castle. As Mike seemed keen to see the Poznan prison camp again, I gave him an afternoon off and my Polish friends took him on his nostalgic trip. The following day I learned that the Polish authorities had preserved the camp in its wartime condition. Photographs of prisoners and guards and original German documents were available for visitors to study. The effect on Mike was unfortunate and unexpected. He suffered a sort of nervous collapse during the night and needed medical attention. When he had recovered, he told me, 'I spent most of the war as a prisoner and I thought it had not affected me badly, but that trip brought it all back to me. It made me quite ill and now I realise that I should not have gone back to that place.' Mike was in his late sixties and I feared that the traumatic experience could have triggered a fatal heart attack. I vowed never again to arrange such a visit for anyone. Escapes from prison camps were nerve-racking experiences and I belatedly realized that Mike did not need someone like me to chide him about his failure to avoid recapture.

After his release from Colditz, Mike returned to his regiment where he was presented with a huge mess bill for the time that he had spent in prison camps.

During the war, my friend Tony Spacek was seconded from the Czech Army to the Royal Air Force as an armaments officer. We both served at the Empire Air Armaments School at Manby in Lincolnshire, but we did not meet there. The frail Tony was sweeping the concrete steps of a block of flats, where he worked as an elderly janitor, when I met him in Prague during the Cold War.

Tony Spacek's series of daring escapes started when Hitler's troops marched into Czechoslovakia. Tony and his fellow members of the Czechoslovak Army had no opportunity to fight when their country was shamefully sold out to Hitler by the British and French appeasers but, when the Germans invaded neighbouring Poland, Tony decided to oppose the Nazis by escaping and joining the western Allies. He travelled to the small village where his mother lived to bid farewell. As he entered the back door of her cottage, his mother warned him that German troops were nearby, so he sneaked out of the cottage, mounted a horse and galloped out of the village. He managed to get over the border into Hungary, only to be immediately arrested by the Hungarians and later put on a train back to Czechoslovakia.

After returning across the Czechoslovak border, the train stopped briefly and Tony scrambled down onto the tracks and sprinted to another train that took him back into Hungary. From Hungary he travelled to Yugoslavia and from there managed to reach France via North Africa. Some of his friends, who had already arrived in France before him, were offered the option of internment or enlistment in the French Foreign Legion. By the time Tony arrived the regular French Army was ready to accept Czech soldiers into its ranks. Tony served with distinction in actions against the Germans and won the Croix de Guerre. When the French Army collapsed under the German onslaught, Tony was obliged to escape once again. The only country where he could continue the fight against the Nazis was Britain, which was under siege and had lost a large part of its army with all its equipment at Dunkirk. He knew that if Britain fell there would be no further escapes. Together with thousands of other Czechoslovak combatants, Tony made the hazardous journey to England and enlisted in our depleted armed forces. Initially, he was selected for training as a parachutist to be dropped in Czechoslovakia as a saboteur but, after parachutist training, he eventually faced the German Army again as a tank commander on the western front. Meanwhile, the military authorities had sent him on an English language course and that is when the dashing Czech officer met Jean, an attractive young officer of the Women's Auxiliary Air Force. It was a case of love at first sight. They married in 1943 and planned to settle in Czechoslovakia after the war.

After their eventual demobilization, Tony returned home and proudly introduced his young bride to his parents. Jean studied the Czech language and settled down to enjoy her new life while Tony continued his military career in the post of Commander of the Presidential Palace Guard. He was about to return to the Staff College in Prague when, in 1948, the communists took control of the country and proceeded to imprison everyone who had served in the British armed forces. Tony hastily began preparations for an escape back to England with Jean and their infant son. However, the Czech authorities blocked his escape, so he told Jean to take the baby and flee without him. He proposed to follow as soon as possible. The communists repeatedly thwarted Jean's attempts to obtain an exit visa and leave the country. At one stage they told her to make an inventory of all the items in her travelling trunk and list the value of each item of clothing. She had bought some garments so long ago that she had forgotten the exact cost, but she presented a list of items with estimated values. The authorities then charged her tax on everything. She had forgotten to list some of her clothes and when she eventually reached safety in England, she discovered that they had been stolen out of the trunk. Clothing was strictly rationed in England at that time, so replacing missing items was extremely difficult.

When Tony was arrested in 1948 he protested his innocence of any crime. The prosecuting authorities pointed out that he was married to an Englishwoman. 'But I have done nothing wrong,' Tony protested. Their reply was, 'Being married to an English wife, you are very likely to do something wrong.' He was sent to prison and Jean wanted to visit him but the British authorities advised her not to risk travelling back to Prague. They suggested that it might help Tony to obtain his release from prison if she divorced him. She wrote and explained the situation to Tony and he was quite understandably distraught but, in due course, the divorce went ahead as suggested. Sadly, it did not help. Tony was sentenced to ten years' imprisonment and sent as a slave worker to the uranium ore mines where he remained for twelve years. After release he was restricted to low grade manual labour for the rest of his working life. The only work offered to him was refuse collecting, but he chose to return to the uranium mine and work there as a poorly paid employee. Out of his meagre wages he managed to save a little and send it to Jean for their young son. Although he was no longer a prisoner, he was denied all civil rights and was unable to travel abroad.

During his first escape, Tony Spacek had shared a Hungarian prison cell with his friend Jan Stursa and, later, they had been prisoners in the uranium ore mines at the same time. They told me that, when totally exhausted, they had sometimes slept on the belts that conveyed the ore. Work in the mines had a detrimental effect on their health for the rest of their lives. On the day I first met Stursa, he was with eight other Czechs and I was the only person present who had not served time in prison. 'Keep tight hold of your wallet,' Stursa quipped. During the war he had worked as an army radio operator at the War Office in London, sending secret messages to agents in enemy-occupied Europe. After training as a parachutist, he was briefed in preparation for his first secret mission. For twenty-four hours before departure he was confined to barracks and forbidden to communicate with anyone outside the camp. Consequently he could not meet his English girlfriend as arranged. He was flown over to Czechoslovakia three times but never dropped. By the time he was allowed out into the local town again, one of his friends had taken his place in his girlfriend's affections and married her. Stursa returned to Prague at the end of the war and, when the communists came to power in 1948, his friends warned him that his arrest was imminent. Like Tony Spacek, he was innocent but he was locked in a cell and interrogated every hour. He was deprived of sleep and prevented from sitting or lying down. His jailers made him keep walking non-stop in his cell. Each time he dropped down from exhaustion he was dragged away and savagely beaten during further interrogations. After three weeks he was able to sleep on his feet. I wondered what the interrogators wanted him to tell them. He said, 'They wanted me to say that I was a spy.' I asked him, 'Were you a spy?' He answered, 'No, I was not, but if I had said "yes" to stop the beatings, they would have shot me.'

After serving his sentence with Tony Spacek in the mines, he was released to work as a labourer on building sites for the rest of his working life. He never recovered completely from his ordeals at the hands of the communists and in later life became a heavy drinker. We were friends until the day he died.

Anna was Jan Stursa's friend for many years. She tried to look after him by cooking his food, attending to his clothes and keeping him off the bottle, but he seemed to resent the fuss. He preferred to live by himself and Anna was fighting a losing battle in trying to help him.

Anna had served on the Eastern Front as a young combat nurse. She told me that one day she had to leave the front line because she was running out of medical supplies and urgently needed bandages. During her quest she came across a group of Russian soldiers. In her less than perfect English, she told me, 'They all loved me. I did not want it, but I could not stop them.' Apparently, they had molested her, but she could not find the right English words to describe the ordeal. Anna was one of thousands of Czech men and women who had fled eastwards away from the Germans and served in Czechoslovak units under Red Army command. Most of the Czechoslovaks who fought on the Eastern Front did not suffer the same post-war persecution as their compatriots who had served in Britain, some of whom scornfully referred to the Eastern Front veterans as 'the Bolsheviks'.

CHAPTER SIX

Although I had not expected to secure any contracts for British equipment, I was surprisingly successful in my dealings with the Communist State Trading Corporations in Prague. When I visited their sparsely-furnished offices during my first brief visit and talked with the ill-clad staff, I doubted that the poor Czechs would be able to afford anything produced in the West, but I was wrong. They welcomed me warmly. I was their first visitor from Britain. As a German- and Russian-speaking production-engineering specialist, I was something of a novelty in a country starved of modern technology. I learned that some American businessmen had visited briefly one morning and flown away in the afternoon, never to return. Within four days of my arrival in Prague, I secured a contract worth £89,000 sterling, which was a great deal of money in those days. It seemed that I would not lack business incentives to continue my trips to Prague. I returned to England and placed my order with a manufacturer in the Midlands; I knew that it had a full order book and long delivery times. Nevertheless, I requested that top priority be given to the Czechoslovak deal because the Czechs had been our wartime Allies. A few weeks later the chairman of the Humber car company visited the factory and noticed rows of machines with instruction plates in Czech. He was most indignant that the Czech machines were being processed ahead of machines ordered by his company and he complained to the production manager who, in turn, mentioned the matter to me. I said, 'He can get stuffed. I think there is more potential business behind the Iron Curtain than we will ever get from the British motorcar industry.' Confident that I was right, I formed a new company for trading exclusively with the communist-controlled countries.

As an independent international trader, I was able to pick and choose my suppliers and I found that my services as an intermediary were in great demand by manufacturers who were not capable of dealing directly in the mysterious world behind the Iron Curtain. After becoming firmly established as a major supplier to Poland and Czechoslovakia, I expanded my sphere of activity to include Hungary, Rumania and Yugoslavia – countries over which I had been active during the air war. Later I added Bulgaria and the DDR (East Germany).

I was wandering through the streets of Warsaw when I saw a brown jacket on sale with a price ticket equivalent to £5 sterling. Thinking that the jacket and an open-neck Polish shirt would help me to merge into the Polish background, I entered the shop and asked the assistant to let me try it on. She asked, 'Do you want to try the trousers too?' I was surprised that it was a complete suit for such a low price. The style was not highly fashionable by western standards, but that would be its advantage as part of my disguise, so I bought it. The material was a little rough and it reminded me of a story that I heard from an acquaintance in West Berlin. He told me that, before the wall divided the city, he went to visit his cousin in the eastern sector. After describing the cousin's poor living standard, he told me that, during a meal, the cousin spilled some meat sauce on the knee of his trousers. His dog licked it off and, in the process, licked a hole right through the leg of the trousers. 'The suit was made of potato fibre,' he told me. 'Everything over there is "ersatz" (substitute) material.' I was sceptical about stories comparing the dreary conditions in the Soviet sector with those in the British and American sectors. In the early post-war years, the West Berliners liked to tell anti-communist stories – especially about the behaviour of Russian soldiers who had never seen modern amenities. Dozens of times I heard that the soldiers allegedly tried to wash their potatoes in an upstairs lavatory pan and after flushing the pan went downstairs to look for them.

One warm summer evening in Prague I put on my Polish clothes, slipped quietly out of the Alcron Hotel and boarded a tram in Vaclavske nameste. I had arranged to meet some former partisans in a quiet district where there was a pub on nearly every street corner. Our rendezvous was at a pub named the 'Good Soldier

Schweik' and I arrived there about fifteen minutes too early, so I settled down to wait at a table on the pavement and ordered '*velke pivo, prosim*' from one of the bustling waiters. I could say things in Czech, although I could not speak the language properly. Fortunately, beer is called '*pivo*' in all Slav languages and I had no difficulty in ordering food and drink wherever I happened to be. Just as the waiter brought my beer, the police arrived and carted several men away in handcuffs. I automatically checked that I was carrying my passport and then asked the nearest Czech what was going on. He explained in halting German that the arrested men were 'potato bandits' who bought up cheap potatoes when they were plentiful and sold them at a higher price later when stocks were scarce. The 'criminals' were budding entrepreneurs who would undoubtedly become successful businessmen if they managed to outlive the communist system.

When the former freedom fighters arrived, we went inside and huddled in a quiet corner. They told me about their wartime exploits as anti-Nazi saboteurs and said, 'If you like, we will take you to the place where the communists murdered our Foreign Minister, Jan Masaryk, shortly after they took power.' I met them again the next afternoon and we went to a building, described to me as the Foreign Ministry, where Masaryk had lived in a first-floor apartment. I was shown the spot where his body was found below his apartment's window. The communist government had reported that he committed suicide by jumping from the window, but my Czech companions maintained that he was thrown out of the window. They said, 'He was in his pyjamas. It is unlikely that he would have bothered to undress if he intended killing himself.' We entered the building and they showed me the window. They said, 'There was evidence of shit on the windowsill. He would not have done that unless he was being murdered.'

My companions had been members of a group of communist partisans during the Nazi occupation. I had supported such groups by dropping supplies to them in various enemy-occupied countries. I was keen to hear their accounts of wartime acts of sabotage but, as they were now members of an anti-Soviet dissidents' group, I was wary of becoming openly involved with them. Incidentally, some people who pretended to be opponents of the communist system were actually police agents, seeking to entrap unsuspecting westerners.

It was said that throwing victims out of windows of high buildings was the most common means of assassination behind the Iron Curtain. It was certainly the cheapest method. In due course, sophisticated methods were developed for use on both sides of the Curtain and they outlasted the Cold War.

For a while I seemed to be fooling the communist police in my Polish clothes but, to my surprise, a uniformed policeman stopped me in Vaslavske namesti and demanded my *Ausweis* (identity document) in fluent German. I asked him how he knew that I was not Czech. He pointed to my feet and said, 'I know you are a foreigner because those are not our kind of shoes.' Obviously I was not as clever as I thought I was. He seemed satisfied when I showed him my British passport with valid business visa, but he must have been surprised to see an English businessman dressed in such cheap clothes. One afternoon the former partisans took me to the street corner where British-trained Czech parachutists had attacked and fatally wounded Heydrich, the hated and feared senior Nazi whom the Czechs labelled the 'Butcher of Prague'. At the time I knew little about Heydrich but, a few years after the war, I became a close friend of the retired Royal Air Force pilot who had conveyed the Czech assassins and dropped them by parachute in their homeland. He was Group Captain Ron Hockey, formerly commander of Number 138 (Special Duties) Squadron, based at Tempsford. The clandestine tasks of the squadron included ferrying secret agents in Hudsons and Lysanders to and from locations in enemy-occupied territory. The squadron initially used Whitleys and, later, Halifaxes to convey secret agents to destinations as far away as Poland. When I asked Ron Hockey about the operation to drop Heydrich's assassins, he shrugged his shoulders, 'I was just the driver.'

From my own experience of similar lone flights to faraway destinations in enemy territory, I know the perils that confronted the 'drivers' and their crews. Since the war much has been written and films have been made about the Czech parachutists who were responsible for the assassination of Heydrich, but few people are aware of the vital part that Ron Hockey and others played in that and many other hazardous secret operations. After learning of the unfortunate fate of the parachutists and the dreadful German revenge that followed the assassination, I wondered why it had been undertaken. I discovered that the British government was unhappy about Czechoslovak factories and workers being harnessed to the German war effort. In turn, the Czechoslovak authorities in exile in London wanted to prove that they were useful allies rather than minor participants in the war against the Nazis.

Whatever the reason might have been, a decision was made to send Czech parachutists to assassinate Heydrich. The officials responsible for the decision must have known that the Germans customarily slaughtered dozens of innocent people as a reprisal every time underground resistance forces killed a single one of their soldiers. They must surely have foreseen the terrible repercussions that would follow the assassination of a senior member of the Nazi hierarchy. Following the death of Heydrich, the Germans began reprisals by killing innocent Czechs each day until they discovered the whereabouts of the parachutists. The men were traced to the crypt of Prague's Church of Saint Cyril and there they died. The Germans then destroyed the villages of Lidice and Lezaky, and slaughtered their entire male populations. One of the inhabitants of Lidice was a woman whose brother was serving on a Czechoslovak squadron of the Royal Air Force in England. Some years later, when I met her in Prague, she told me that other women in Lidice had savagely turned on her and said, 'Your cursed brother and his RAF colleagues are the cause of our suffering.' They were wrong. The British authorities and the Czechoslovak exile government were the ones responsible for the fiasco. It caused endless suffering and did nothing to shorten the war. The Czech parachutists have been hailed rightly as heroes, but the episode was just another wartime example of idiotic decisions and wasted lives. The brave parachutists would have been far more usefully engaged on industrial sabotage.

During a visit to the crypt where the parachutists died, I saw that the Czechs had turned it into a memorial to them. There were photographs of German troops shooting into the crypt and of fire hoses being used to flood the parachutists' refuge. When I mentioned to Ron Hockey that there were no photographs or documents relating to the role of the Royal Air Force, he said that he would assemble a collection of suitable material about Number 138 Squadron and present it to the Czechs one day. Despite being terminally ill with bone cancer, he made the brave decision to travel to Prague towards the end of the Cold War. He visited the crypt and presented photographs and a commemorative copper plaque to the priest in charge. The plaque incorporated an engraved dedication and an applied copy of 138 Squadron's official badge. The next time I visited the crypt I saw that the plaque was firmly fixed to the interior wall of the crypt. Sadly, someone had prised off and stolen the squadron's badge. Ron Hockey was nearing the end of his life and I did not have the heart to tell him about the shameful vandalism that I presume was the work of a visiting souvenir hunter.

CHAPTER SEVEN

When visiting Poland during the early days of the Cold War, I met scores of Polish men and women who had fought in the Armia Krajowa, but I had difficulty in finding Poles who had served in the Royal Air Force because so many of them were serving long prison sentences or were lying low after being released.

One day I stopped my car in a small village and wandered through the market. I watched horses dragging rustic crates along the road. As the crates bumped over the cobblestones into the market place, I saw that each one contained a squealing pig. Old women in long dresses and headscarves squatted on upturned boxes beside piles of unwashed root vegetables, cardboard trays of tiny yellow ducklings and boxes of multi-coloured chicks. Among scores of horse-drawn carts there was one solitary tractor and I saw the driver staring at my Rover car with its GB plate. When I approached, he told me in good English that he had been a bomber pilot at RAF Waddington near Lincoln. He returned home at the end of the war, intending to take over the large family farm from his elderly parents, but the communist authorities commandeered the property and he now worked there as a poorly-paid tractor driver. His face lit up as he spoke wistfully about wartime trips to Nottingham's Palais de Dance and drinks in the Blackboys pub. I was sorry to see him in such reduced circumstances, unshaven and in shabby clothes, but he was lucky to have survived twice as many bombing operations as I had done. He seemed keen to detain me for a long chat, but I explained that I was just passing through on my way to Poznan and I had merely stopped for a few minutes to stretch my legs. I later regretted not asking him his name.

When he mentioned the Nottingham Palais de Dance, I remembered how the dance hall was a favourite haunt of the Polish airmen. They were successful in charming our English girls but, due to their poor command of our language, their intentions were sometimes misunderstood. A British officer of the Provost's Department told me with a smile, 'An indignant Englishwoman complained to the police that a Polish airman had made improper suggestions to her and she told him that she was a good woman.' He replied, 'Yes, you are very good woman. I am very good man. We can make very good time together. Okay?' When questioned in Polish by his superiors, he explained that he was merely trying to ask her for a date.

Olive was a Nottingham girl who secretly attended the afternoon sessions at the Palais de Dance. Her father warned her not to go there, 'The place is full of bloody foreigners. You stay away from there, my girl.' Olive's life became complicated when she met a handsome Polish pilot at the Palais and fell in love with him. While her father was at work, she took him home to meet her mother. She told me:

> My mother thought he was lovely with his bowing and hand kissing – especially when he brought her flowers, but when father heard about him he warned, 'If you bring him here, I'll shoot the bugger.' father could not tolerate foreigners.

Olive continued her secret romance with the connivance of her mother who eventually told father, 'For goodness sake, stop being so pig-headed. It would not do any harm to meet the fellow. Olive will not give him up, no matter what you say.' After Mother had squared up father, he reluctantly allowed Olive to bring her Polish pilot home for afternoon tea. Olive was on tenterhooks as she waited for father to come home from work and hoped he would not be hostile to her friend. When father arrived, Olive told him, 'This is my friend Joe. He is a flying instructor at RAF Newton.' Joe looked immaculate in his uniform and Olive felt so proud of him. He jumped to his feet as father approached, extended his hand and said, 'I have been looking forward to the pleasure of meeting you sir.' Olive told me, 'My father took to Joe as soon as he said he wanted to stay in England after the war. I was the only daughter and father had been worried that the "bloody foreigner" would take me abroad if we got married. And I think he was pleased when Joe kept calling him sir.' They did marry and, after the war, Joe, the former pilot, got a job as a labourer in a local lace factory. The factory supervisor was the man who had cleaned Joe's aeroplane during the war.

After some time Joe was promoted from sweeping the factory floor to a more important job in the lace-making industry. A few years later the factory manager told Joe, 'I want you to take my son under your wing and train him.' After Joe had taught the manager's son everything, he became Joe's boss. 'Oh well, that's life,' Joe told me. He remained in the Nottingham lace industry until he retired and then he made a couple of compassionate trips to visit his elderly relatives behind the Iron Curtain. The officials of certain Polish émigré organizations in Britain expressed their strong disapproval of such visits and threatened to withdraw club membership from people such as Joe.

I discovered that some of the people who managed the émigré clubs were embittered old men who originated in the part of Poland that had been incorporated into the Soviet Union. If those men had wanted to visit their own relatives, the Soviet authorities would not have granted permission. For many years I avoided contact with the embittered Polish émigrés, but I was well aware that they secretly disapproved of my commercial contact with the people they called 'the communists'. What the émigré Poles did not know was that, in forty years of travel in the communist-controlled countries, I met many opportunists, but nobody who I would describe as a true communist. The communist idealists were either incarcerated in gulags and lunatic asylums or exiled abroad. I associated with many members of the Communist Party's hierarchy behind the Iron Curtain and I am sure that such people always scrambled to the top, regardless of the political system. Among manual workers, there were Socialists, just as in Britain, but I never met anyone in the Soviet satellite countries who expressed approval of the Russian brand of communism. Moreover, nobody ever tried to thrust communist dogma at me.

During a particularly harsh winter's day, the officials of the state trading corporation, Metalexport, invited me to visit a factory near

Warsaw. The factory was a collection of wooden shacks and I arrived there during a snowstorm. I met the factory director who was dressed in a fur coat and a leather flying helmet. I hoped he might be an ex-aviator but, as he understood little English, I realized that he was not an ex-RAF man. The snow was blowing almost horizontally as we ran from one workshop to another. My feet and fingers were numb as I watched men in the assembly workshop clipping steel panels onto a telescopic wooden frame and welding them together. They were building a motor car. The director said, 'Please don't laugh at our methods.' I replied, 'I am not laughing. I am amazed that you can make cars in such primitive conditions.' He explained that they only made official cars, one at a time, for the top communist bosses. He said, 'If we need to make a longer car, we extend the wooden frame and insert another panel.' He continued, 'The government wants us to develop a modern motor car plant, but we don't know where to start. We never see a machinery catalogue. We don't know what kind of equipment we need and we lack the technology. Can you help us?' I told him that I was a major supplier of machinery to the automotive industry in Detroit where I had a branch office and to all the car manufacturers in Britain. I would be happy to help him. I said, 'If you can get the money, I can tell you what you need and if you buy through me you will get the technology thrown in. In our business, what you need is called the know-how.' He was delighted and so was I. As we stood talking in the freezing cold workshop, we were at the start of what would eventually develop into a multi-million pound business.

When officials of the state trading corporations learned of my wartime flights to Warsaw, some of them gave me information on the whereabouts of Polish veterans of the RAF. An official, who was an Armia Krajowa veteran, said, 'Do you know that Skalski is living in Warsaw? I can give you his address, if you like.' I had never heard of Skalski before but, on learning that he was a former RAF pilot, I decided to contact him the next time I came to Warsaw. First, I had to make some enquiries in London to find out about him. In searching through various air force documents, I discovered that Stanislaw Skalski was already an experienced pilot when the

Germans attacked Poland in 1939 and he took part in air combat during the short period before the Luftwaffe overwhelmed his country. He escaped through Rumania and joined in the defence of France before fleeing to England and enlisting in the Royal Air Force in time for the Battle of Britain. Subsequently, he flew against the Germans and Italians during the North African and Italian campaigns. He became the Commanding Officer of the British 601 (County of London) Auxiliary Air Force Squadron. He was the only Polish member of 601 Squadron and yet he was the commander! When I telephoned and asked to meet him, he invited me to lunch in his modest Warsaw apartment where we dined on pike – a fish that I had never tasted before. I noticed his large framed display of personal medals hanging in the hallway and I was keen to learn about his wartime achievements, but he seemed reluctant to talk about the war. However, I discovered that he was particularly proud of his time in command of 601 Squadron.

At that stage of the Cold War, the people behind the Iron Curtain lacked many things that were readily available in the western world. I always took a supply of ball pens, bars of chocolate, magazines and other 'luxury' items to distribute to my business and private contacts. Noticing Skalski's poor standard of living, I asked if he would like me to bring anything for him on my next visit. I half expected him proudly to decline my offer, but he asked me to bring him an official gold-wire badge of 601 Squadron to wear on his blazer. Back in London, I discovered that the Auxiliary Air Force had become the Royal Auxiliary Air Force. I took a 601 Squadron Royal Auxiliary Air Force badge and gave it to him on my next visit. He was thrilled with it and then I gradually learned a little more about him. Although he had had the opportunity to remain in the Royal Air Force at the end of the war, he chose to return to Poland and resume his career in the Polish Air Force. At the start of the Cold War, the communists arrested him on a false charge of spying for the western capitalists. A death sentence was later commuted to life imprisonment. After seven years he was released from prison and his obsession with flying led to his return to service in the Polish Air Force, where he had the opportunity to fly the latest Russian MiG fighter planes and eventually reached the rank of general.

His loyalty was clearly to his Polish homeland, not to the Stalinist regime that had so cruelly persecuted him. Flying was his life-long passion, the only occupation that he knew, but it eventually caused him to be ostracized by some members of the Polish émigré community in Britain who cruelly accused him of 'going over to the communists' and told him that, if ever he came to London, he would not be welcome at the Polish Air Force Club. From my conversations with him, I regarded him as a true Polish patriot with distinct pro-British feelings. In the early days of the Second World War, heroic fighter pilots like Skalski had been an inspiration to me and to a multitude of other young men who were obsessed with flying, and keen to get into the air at all costs.

During my business visits to Warsaw, I often drove past the airfield where German Stuka dive-bombers had taken off for five-minute flights to bomb Warsaw during the 1944 Uprising. I understood that there were only about three Stukas, but they bombed so frequently that the inhabitants of Warsaw thought that there were many more. I remembered that as I was dropping my first load of supplies for the Armia Krajowa on the night of 13 August 1944, I saw several of our Liberators shot down. One of them crash-landed after two of its engines were knocked out and all the instruments stopped working. On my next visit to Krakow, I would tell Zak about the young South African pilot, Lieutenant Robert Klette, who managed to put his plane down in an open space that happened to be the airfield. After his mixed British and South African crew scrambled out of the plane, the Luftwaffe ground personnel opened fire and killed one man – Warrant Officer H. J. Brown. The German action contrasted sharply with the gallant behaviour of First World War airmen of both sides, who were known to show respect for their adversaries. The same attitude had continued during the very early days of the Second World War. I knew from my father, who served as a senior officer, that the Royal Air Force granted the pomp of military funerals with guards of honour for the corpses of enemy airmen. My father ensured that the undertaker sorted and matched up all scattered body parts correctly. When he told me that detached hands, feet and heads usually remained intact, I immediately used an indelible pencil to write my name and number on the suede lining of my flying helmet.

It is commonly understood that truth is the first casualty of war. Sadly, respect for enemy combatants was an early casualty too. By the time I entered the fray, Hitler had instructed the German police and soldiers not to interfere with 'the justifiable wrath of the people'. Consequently, many shot-down and defenceless young Allied airmen were denied their rights as prisoners of war and mauled to death by irate civilians. For us there were no cyanide pills for a quick and easy death – just an unlimited supply of Benzedrine pills to keep us alert on long flights. We knew nothing about the adverse effects of such amphetamines, commonly referred to as pep pills or 'wakey-wakey' tablets.

The transformation from winter to summer came abruptly in Poland and I drove in pleasant sunshine on the fast road to Katowice. After visiting the steelworks, I planned to meet my friend Zak in Krakow where he would show me the plaque marking the site where my flight commander's plane was shot down in August 1944. There was no speed limit on the long straight road and I was clocking around 120mph when an approaching carthorse bolted off the adjacent sand track and crossed the road ahead of me. I saw the driver lean back on his seat and desperately haul on the reins, but to no avail. The horse was out of control. Fortunately, I was able to stop in time and, as the horse galloped past me, I resolved to drive slower on that road in future.

After my business appointment in Katowice, I picked up Zak in Krakow and we made a quick visit to the war cemetery where I photographed some air force graves that I had missed last time. Then Zak guided me to an industrial area where I parked my car next to a factory wall bearing the memorial plaque. I stood reading the names of Liversidge, my former flight commander and his crew. I explained to Zak that the dead men were among the most experienced crews on the squadron. My own less experienced crew had flown over Krakow four times. We had met intense opposition from German fighter planes and we were fortunate to have survived. 'Just the luck of the draw. It could so easily have been my crew on that plaque,' I told Zak.

I started to take some photographs and Zak whispered nervously, 'I have seen a woman looking at us through the window of a building on the other side of the street and now she is speaking on the telephone. I think you should not be taking photographs here. She might be reporting us to the police.'

I said, 'I have finished now. I will just load another film and then we can go.'

I opened the car boot and threw the exposed film into a box containing half a dozen others and, at that moment, two factory policemen appeared. Zak was now in a panic as he interpreted for me, 'They want to take your film away because photography is forbidden here. We are in trouble now. They say you are breaking the law.'

I said, 'Tell them I have only photographed that plaque. Say it bears the names of my Royal Air Force friends who were killed while flying to help the Polish underground army.'

Zak began a long tirade in Polish. He became red-faced and anxious. The factory police looked unimpressed and one of them went back into the factory. Zak told me, 'He has gone to telephone the criminal police. We are in real trouble now.'

When two men in civilian clothes arrived in an ancient motor car, I decided to deal directly with them in German. I was sure that I could manage without Zak's panicky involvement and, furthermore, I wanted to prevent them from bullying him. In situations where it is necessary to be indignant, quarrelsome and arrogant, my preferred language has always been German. I greeted the men brusquely to indicate that I would tolerate no nonsense from them and they explained that they wanted to take away my film. I asked them what they intended to do with it. They said they would develop it to see if it contained sensitive material.

I told them, 'I use colour film. You have no equipment for processing colour. If you try to develop it, you will ruin it and you will not know what was on it.'

They said, 'You have photographed a state factory where secret products are made.'

I laughed, 'I know exactly what is made here, because I supplied much of the equipment that is used by the factory.'

I turned to Zak, 'The factory is part of a large combine. They have bought a lot of stuff from me.'

Zak was not listening. 'They think you are a spy,' he whispered, 'Tell them that you have permission to research the archives at Auschwitz and then they will know that you are important.'

'Certainly not,' I replied, 'That is no business of theirs and I am not making any apologies for photographing that plaque.'

I turned to the policemen and handed them a card, 'If you want to check up on me, I suggest you telephone this man's number in Warsaw. He is the son of the party chairman.'

They turned away murmuring quietly to each other. Their attitude changed from officious to genial. 'It will not be necessary to telephone, but we really do need to take a film.'

I opened the car boot and selected a film at random. They saluted and returned to their car.

As I drove off, I said to Zak, 'There is an English saying: it is not what you know, it is who you know that's important.' He was still uneasy. He had been firmly convinced that we would both end up in gaol.

In the communist dictatorships, where the state ruled over everything, people were not only afraid of the police, they were afraid of each other. Every policeman had about twenty unpaid informers and consequently people tended to be excessively deferential to anyone with a tiny bit of power. Some car-park attendants and junior clerks behaved like police officers. I found that the most effective way to cope with such objectionable people was to shock them by bellowing at them in very loud German.

When dealing with officials behind the Iron Curtain, it was customary to give them a business card and I always carried a few cards inside my English driving licence booklet in the top pocket of my jacket. As I drove Zak to his home, I said, 'There is something puzzling me. Whenever I produce my driving licence to take out a card, people react strangely.'

Zak looked at the small red booklet, 'No wonder they react to it. It is the same size and colour as the Communist Party members' card. Party members are powerful people. As you are an Englishman, they are surprised to see that you have a card.'

I was glad that I had mentioned the matter to Zak. I said, 'Well, you live and learn! I have never seen a party card, so I did not know that my English driving licence looked like one. I will keep it out of sight in future.'

When we reached his home Zak showed me a map on which he had marked sites where Royal Air Force planes were shot down over Poland during the war. In some cases he had listed the names of the crews. There were a few names missing and I agreed to provide them later, after I had perused official documents at the Public Records Office in London. Zak told me that he wanted to find out about other men who flew to Warsaw, but were not shot down over Poland. He asked, 'Did they all get safely back to Italy?' I told him:

> Sadly, not all of them survived. After leaving Poland, they had a long flight over German-occupied Hungary, Czechoslovakia and Yugoslavia. I have visited their graves in the war cemeteries of Prague and Budapest. And some men were killed later while bombing various targets or mining the Danube, so there were not many 'Warsaw crews' left at the end of the war.

Zak pressed me for more information about the survivors and I said:

> Some planes returned to base with dead and wounded on board, but we did not hear much about other squadrons' casualties. In those days, our main concern was our own survival and, although it sounds callous, we didn't take much interest in the fate of anyone who was not a fellow crew member or close personal friend. Most of what we learned about crews of the other squadrons in our group was from gossip in the NAAFI at Foggia. We never got any official information.

I told Zak that it was in the NAAFI that I heard about a South African Air Force Liberator pilot named Senn who was very seriously wounded when his plane was hit by flak over Warsaw.

The navigator and mid-upper gunner were both wounded and damage to the plane made it difficult to control. In spite of a painful leg wound, the pilot managed to nurse the crippled plane all the way back from Warsaw and land it at Celone. Seven aircraft had taken off for Warsaw from Celone that night. Three of them were shot down and three returned with flak damage. The Polish flight at Brindisi suffered the highest percentage of losses and damage, but it was a long time before we found out about that.

At the height of the Warsaw Uprising, Liberator KG927 of the Polish Flight arrived at 300 feet over Warsaw with a load of supplies for the Armia Krajowa. By the time it reached the designated drop zone, the plane was down to 100 feet, and flying through intense 20mm flak and machine-gun bullets. Evasive action was impossible at such a low altitude and the plane was hit repeatedly. Although hampered by the glare of searchlights, the crew managed to release their load of supplies over the drop zone before climbing to 300 feet to clear the city's tallest ruined buildings. Turning away from the burning city, still at 300 feet, the pilot attempted to gain further height, but all the engines failed to respond to the throttle controls. The port outer engine was severely damaged and needed to be feathered to prevent fire, but the feathering system did not work. The plane was flying at normal cruising revolutions and the only way to gain height was to switch to fine propeller pitch. This action increased the airspeed and allowed the plane to climb slowly to 800 feet.

The flight engineer checked the damage to the plane and found that the two huge bomb doors were jammed open. He managed to close one door manually, but the other one would not budge. The manifold pressure gauges and artificial horizon instrument were not working, and the rear gun turret was completely wrecked. Miraculously, although the plane was so seriously damaged, only one crewman was wounded. By the time the plane reached the heavily defended region of Krakow, it had climbed to only 4,000 feet and, in bright moonlight, was an ideal target for fighter planes and flak gunners. Flying slowly on three engines and at high engine revolutions, it made such a deafening noise that the ground defences were alerted long before it appeared overhead. A burst of flak hit the flaps near the fuselage, rendering them useless. The plane was hit again at the rear of the bomb bay and then another burst missed the rear gunner by just a few inches.

When a further burst of flak hit the starboard inner engine it burst into flames and the plane was now flying on only two engines and slowly losing height. The flight engineer warned that the plane might not have enough fuel to reach its base in southern Italy, but the crew decided to stay in the air as long as possible and risk ditching in the Adriatic. After repeatedly re-checking the fuel, the flight engineer finally estimated that, with only two engines running, the plane might just about reach its home base at Brindisi. The radio had been hit, but the Identification Friend or Foe (IFF) was in order, so the radio operator contacted base on the emergency frequency and warned of a possible crash landing.

Miraculously, the plane did reach its Italian base before the fuel ran out. Two crew members managed to lower the undercarriage and the pilot brought the plane down onto the runway at the exceptionally high speed of 160mph with no control over the throttles. After touchdown, an attempt was made to switch off the ignition, but as the engines were so hot they continued running and, although the brake pressure gauges showed a normal reading, the brakes failed to work and the plane, headed for the sea at the end of the runway. By applying extreme pressure on the right rudder pedal, the Polish pilot and co-pilot managed to turn the plane off the runway onto soft ground and, after slewing around 160 degrees, it shuddered to a stop within a few yards of the sea. Finally, as the crew were scrambling out of the plane another one of the engines burst into flames. Other Polish crews had similar horrifying experiences. Many of them discovered after landing that their parachute packs had been shot to pieces. I knew that my friend Zak would be particularly interested in reports about the Polish airmen's efforts to aid the Armia Krajowa. No such information was publicly available in Poland during the Cold War.

We arrived at Zak's home in the late afternoon and he invited me to stay the night. 'There is something I would like you to do for me,' he said. After dinner we went down into the cellar where I noticed a pile of political leaflets. Possession of printing and duplicating equipment was against the law. I knew that if the authorities discovered those things he would be imprisoned and I realized why he had seemed so anxious during our earlier encounter with the police. He produced a pistol from somewhere in the cellar and said, 'Part of the trigger mechanism is missing. It is quite a common gun. I wonder if you would be able to get a replacement part for me in England or the United States.' I said, 'I'm sorry Zak, but the answer is no. I cannot become involved in anything like that.' He was still a partisan at heart and I admired his courage, but I knew that I should neither assist nor encourage him in his illegal activities. We corresponded for a while after that episode, but seldom met again.

The Royal Air Force was never short of aircrew applicants during the Second World War, but not all were accepted. Some were not up to the required physical and educational standards, but my friend Freddie Kessel was turned down for a different reason. He was a Viennese university student on what is now known as a gap year in the spring of 1939. Wanting to see a bit more of the world, he joined the crew of a tramp steamer in the temporary capacity of writer. The ship sailed from port to port, picking up and putting down cargo. It had no radio, so the crew were out of touch with world events until they eventually reached the port of Liverpool and discovered that war had been declared. Freddie, who knew no English, was hauled off to the local police station and locked in a cell. Early the next morning he had his first introduction to the English language when a policeman entered the cell with a can of tea and told him to produce his mug. Freddie did not understand what was required of him so he just looked puzzled. The Liverpool policeman bellowed impatiently, 'Yer moog – yer bloody moog. Where's yer bloody moog?'

Shortly after this incident the authorities registered the rather bewildered Freddie as an enemy alien and shipped him off to an internment camp in Australia, where he expected to remain confined for the rest of the war. However, he was told that he would be released and returned to England, if he agreed to join the British Army. He agreed but, after he reached England, nobody took any further interest in him so he spent a few days sightseeing in London while brushing up his English. Needing money, he went to the Labour Exchange and asked for work. The clerk gave him a document to take to a factory and there he was told to enter his personal details on a form. When the factory manager saw that Freddie's place of birth was Vienna, he exclaimed, 'You can't work here. We are engaged on work for the Ministry of Aircraft Production. It is all secret stuff. You had better go back to the Labour Exchange and tell them we can't take you.'

Freddie realized that all the factories were engaged on war work, so he informed the officials at the Labour Exchange that he had been released from internment to join the Army. While at the Labour Exchange, he saw a poster urging men to 'Fly with the Royal Air Force', so he filled in the appropriate application form. A RAF warrant officer checked the form and told him, 'You can't join the Air Force. If you were a pilot, you might be told to bomb places in Austria!'

Freddie was disappointed. He would have preferred to be a pilot rather than an ordinary soldier and he certainly would not have objected to bombing the Nazis. After being handed over to an Army recruiting sergeant, he was enlisted in the Intelligence Corps. During the later stages of the war he was engaged in the interrogation of captured senior German officers. When a German general heard him speaking faultless German, he asked him where he learned the language. 'You studied German at the university, I suppose?' Freddie replied dismissively, 'Oh no; just at ordinary school.' As a British Army sergeant, he was not prepared to disclose his origin to the Germans. I knew nothing about the wartime activities of the British Army's Intelligence Corps and Freddie did little to enlighten me. However, he did reveal that members of the Corps and their American opposite numbers advanced into Germany ahead of the main body of Allied troops. One of their tasks was to collect secret Nazi documents and other items of particular importance and protect them from looters. He told me:

> One day, our Jeeps pulled up in front of a German field marshal's château. The elderly housekeeper announced, 'The field marshal has gone. His car is in the garage – take it.

Nobody is here except the servants. Take the car, but please do not harm us.' We told her that we were not interested in the car, but we intended searching the premises. We entered the field marshal's study, opened the desk drawers and examined various items of correspondence. The housekeeper pleaded, 'Please do not take any documents away. They are not important – they are just letters from President Hindenburg.' We told her that, as they were of no importance, it would not matter what became of them and we gathered them up, and took them with us. I suppose they are now somewhere in a private collection or in a museum with other interesting German documents.

The war ended and Freddie was on demobilization leave in his London lodgings. Still dressed in his British Army uniform with sergeant's stripes and British medal ribbons, he opened the door in response to loud knocking by a police sergeant. After checking Freddie's identity, the police sergeant said, 'We have been informed that you are an enemy alien. In accordance with the regulations, you must report at the police station each week and you must notify us of any change of address.'

Some years later Freddie spoke impeccable English. He now had British nationality and was a university lecturer on international law. He had developed the persona of a typical English gentleman with upper-class accent and a new name. He told me that, during the run-up to the general election, he had canvassed for a British political party in his spare time. He called at a London flat where the inhabitant berated him with, 'It's an absolute disgrace. The bloody foreigners are getting all the new council houses.' Freddie chuckled as he told me, 'The man would have been surprised if he had known that he was talking to a former 'bloody foreigner' whose first introduction to the English language was, where's yer bloody moog?'

As mentioned, the Royal Air Force turned Freddie down because of his Austrian nationality, but some other Austrians and Germans did serve as pilots in our air force. During my time in Italy I met men of our tactical close support squadrons. Those squadrons and the strategic heavy bomber squadrons were mainly staffed by a mixture of men from Britain, Canada, Australia, New Zealand, South Africa and other parts of the British Empire. I had not expected to find any Germans but, at the aircrew disposal centre near Naples, I was chatting to an English pilot when I noticed a pilot with the label 'Palestine' on his shoulder. I made enquiries and discovered that the man was one of several pilots of German birth. I asked my English companion, 'What are they like?' He replied with a laugh, 'You would not want to fly with them. They are bloody crazy. They don't just bomb the target like the rest of us. After bombing, they go down low and strafe it like hell.'

In time, I came across several other foreign pilots who conducted a private vendetta against the enemy in addition to carrying out official instructions. They were not the only ones. My squadron's bomb-aimers could set the Liberator's bomb selector instrument so that all except one bomb fell on the designated target and one bomb was saved for a target of their own choice. On the way back to base the bomb-aimers might drop that spare bomb on a flak battery that had been particularly troublesome. This sort of action was strictly against the rules, of course.

One night I was crossing the Danube on the way back to base after bombing railway marshalling yards in northern Hungary. Suddenly, an enemy plane shot down a Liberator within a couple of hundred yards of us. As soon as the Liberator had hit the ground in flames and exploded, I saw a runway light up briefly while the enemy plane landed. On that occasion I wished that I had saved a bomb for such an ideal 'target of opportunity'.

After completing my tour on Number 178 Liberator Squadron at Amendola, I spent a few weeks at the Portici aircrew disposal centre near Naples where I met Flight Sergeant Snow, who had just completed his tour on one of the tactical bomber squadrons. Snow told me that the close support squadrons were based so close to the front line that they sometimes arrived over their targets within five minutes of taking off and crews were advised to wear their steel helmets in the air during low-level bombing attacks. Some navigator/bomb-aimers did not wear their tin hats on their heads; they preferred to use them to protect their genitals when lying down during the bombing run. Other men, who did wear their tin hats on their heads, used their bulky parachute packs to protect their most precious parts. When a number of planes mysteriously blew up while taking off, sabotage was at first suspected, but then it was found that enemy agents hiding in the long grass were throwing sticky bombs at them as they passed low overhead.

When Snow's plane was badly damaged by anti-aircraft fire the other members of his crew were severely wounded. While struggling to control the plane, he could do nothing to help them and they bled to death. He was unhurt physically, but his inability to help his dying friends still haunted him long after he left the squadron.

The expression 'post-traumatic stress syndrome' had not yet come into use and, instead of receiving counselling, aircrews faced unjust charges of cowardice if they cracked up under the stress of combat. I am reminded that in the 1914-18 war pilots were denied the use of parachutes to ensure that they did not jump out under fire and some soldiers faced a firing squad to deter others from breaking down. Although no men were shot at dawn in the Second World War, the callous attitude of many of our leaders continued unchanged.

Clearly, being a member of a defeated force was even worse than being one of the victors (and that was bad enough), so I took every opportunity of talking to German veterans about their wartime experiences.

Director Krellman, who had served as an artillery officer on the Eastern Front, was one of my frequent business visitors to London and we became firm friends. He spoke no English. One evening we were chatting at the bar of a London pub when he glanced suspiciously at people standing near us and whispered anxiously, 'Is it alright to be speaking German here?' The war had already been over for about five years, but I could understand his concern. I told him that there were no secret agents listening to us and most English people would not recognize the language anyway. After living so long in a police state, he had not yet become accustomed to speaking freely in public. He was among the first Germans to tell me about conditions on the Eastern Front. He said:

> We had plenty of ammunition and we were still firing when we were overrun by Russian infantrymen who advanced regardless of losses in such huge numbers that we could not shoot them all. They did not stop to capture us; they just kept running like crazy in the direction of Berlin. After the first wave of infantry, the support troops raced past us and we saw that they had no guns – just rolled blankets slung over their shoulders. Very soon we were isolated and there was nobody left to shoot, so we just packed up and tried to get back to Germany alive.

Incidentally, Krellman seemed to have an odd sense of humour. Sometimes I wondered if he really had any sense of humour at all. He described himself as a part-time judge and, although I did not understand the German legal system, I guessed that he was some sort of magistrate. One day he told me of a recent case that came before his court. It concerned a girl who had bitten off the end of a man's penis. Another girl told the court that the accused girl had often expressed the intention of doing such a thing if ever she got an opportunity. On hearing the story, I said, 'I bet that took a bit of explaining when he got home.' Krellman replied dryly, 'Fortunately, he died.' I could not help smiling at that remark.

Knowing that I had served in the Royal Air Force, my friend Krellman kept me supplied with German books, such as one by Galland, the chief of the Luftwaffe's fighter force. From Galland I learned that German aircrews were treated even worse by their high command than we were by ours. Hitler and Göring were angered by the successes of the Royal Air Force and accused their own pilots of cowardly reluctance to press home attacks on Allied bombers. They told their pilots that they did not deserve the gallantry awards that they had 'gained by swindle'. Galland suspended the wearing of his own decorations as a protest against the criticism of his men and when asked by Göring what he needed to beat the Royal Air Force he famously replied, 'Give me a squadron of British Spitfires.'

Before the war, the RAF pilot Douglas Bader lost his legs in a crash while showing off to people on the ground. Flying with 'tin legs', he became an ace fighter pilot during the war. When he was shot down, Galland courteously entertained him in the German officers' mess. Bader asked to meet the German pilot who had shot him down and was disappointed to find that the man was a relatively inexperienced corporal. After the war, the initially resentful Bader became friendly with Galland. Bader occasionally flew very low over my Sussex farm in a helicopter when visiting my ex-RAF neighbour, who, like Bader, had connections with oil companies. I wondered if Bader's friend Galland was on board the helicopter as it swooped down to land in a nearby field, scattering my horses, sheep and poultry in the process. I climbed up my granary steps and aimed a walking stick like a rifle at the machine, childishly pretending to shoot it down. I imagined Bader and his passenger asking my neighbour, 'Why does the strange fellow at the neighbouring farm aim a gun at us?' In reply to a similar question from my wife, I joked, 'They are violating my airspace.'

CHAPTER EIGHT

On a warm afternoon I was driving along the picturesque Rhineland highway between Bingen and Bonn. I had been at the wheel for about ten hours when I pulled off the road and drank from a bottle of mineral water. I noticed that I was near a small engineering factory, so I drove into the car park and got out to stretch my legs. A man in overalls approached and, obviously assuming that I was a visitor, directed me to the reception office. I was surprised to discover an engineering factory in such a picturesque location and thought I might as well find out what was being produced there. A woman in the front office invited me to wait in the director's office. 'He is in the workshop,' she told me in German, 'He will be back in a minute.' As I waited I noticed two small black-framed photographs of young airmen in smart German uniforms on the wall behind the desk. I thought that the black frames signified that they were dead and I might be about to meet their grieving father. When the director arrived I told him that I was an English importer and we chatted amicably. I asked him if he owned the factory and he said, 'I do now. I acquired it at the end of the war when the former owner was killed.'

He obviously wanted to talk, so I listened quietly as he continued:

I was the factory manager throughout the war. We were engaged on essential war work and told to increase output. We were short of workers until loads of foreign prisoners were sent to us. They were mostly Yugoslavs and we accommodated them in huts in a barbed-wire compound next to the factory. Although they were prisoners, they were not badly treated by the factory owner. After all, we relied on them to maintain our monthly production quota and we were in trouble with the authorities if output fell.

I asked him about the factory owner. 'You said he was killed. How did that happen?' He explained:

It was very tragic. His two boys had already been killed a year before the Allies arrived here. The first troops were aggressive, young trigger-happy Americans. They nearly scared me to death. They lined everybody up at gunpoint and demanded to know which of us was SS or Gestapo. Suddenly, one of the Yugoslav workers pointed at me and shouted, 'He is Gestapo'. I was not a member of the Gestapo, but I had to make a report every month about any worker who was disobedient or slacking, so I was not exactly popular. When the man shouted that I was Gestapo I thought my end had come, but he immediately fell down in an epileptic fit, so I rushed over to him and shoved a piece of a stick into his mouth to prevent him biting off his tongue. The ensuing confusion diverted attention away from me and that probably saved my life, but the factory owner was not so lucky.

I said, 'I hope the Americans did not shoot him.' He replied:

Oh no. They did not shoot anybody and, after they left, the boss told me to open the gates of the compound and let the Yugoslavs out. Some of them got hold of some schnapps and got drunk, and then one went to the factory owner's house and asked to see him. The maid let him into the house and, when the owner appeared, the Yugoslav produced a pistol and shot the poor man dead. As I said before, we had not treated the men badly. I can understand their anger about being taken from their homes and sent here as slave workers, but it was not our fault. The authorities allocated them to us and we could not refuse to take them. I still have a couple of Yugoslavs here who did not want to go back. They are good workers and I am glad they stayed. Luckily, nobody shot me and, as there were no family members left to inherit the factory, it eventually passed into my possession.

The director's description of the arrival of the first American troops was similar to accounts by other Germans. Apparently, it was a common occurrence for SS and Gestapo people to be shot out of hand by the first troops to enter a town. I heard that, in one place, all the members of the local fire brigade were shot when their dark-blue uniforms caused them to be mistaken for SS men. Blunders were commonplace and inevitable in the general confusion of front-line actions. I met some former Luftwaffe pilots who surrendered to American troops in Croatia. The Americans, described as very angry young men, ordered the German airmen, in such an aggressive manner, to line up with their hands on their heads that they feared that they were about to be shot on the spot. The German airmen eventually realized that their captors were just as jittery as they were, but were not about to kill them.

My friend Karl Feist was an Austrian who managed several companies from his offices in Vienna. We met by chance when both competing for the same contract in Czechoslovakia and we decided to join forces. Thereafter, we worked together for several years in Czechoslovakia and Hungary. Karl's attitude was similar to mine. He was willing to sell, without prejudice, to anyone who had money. During his first visit to my offices in London, he told me that he was conscripted into the German army at the beginning of the war and sent to France where he joined other soldiers preparing to invade England. He said, 'I had seen pictures of the sights of London in tourist brochures, and I was looking forward to seeing the Tower of London and all the other famous places.'

He and his young fellow soldiers waited excitedly for their boat trip to England and they were dismayed when the invasion was cancelled, and they ended up on the Eastern Front instead. 'Contrary to our fears and expectations, however, it was wonderful at first,' he told me:

> The anti-communist people in the Ukraine welcomed us like heroes. They greeted us with the traditional gifts of bread and salt, and gave us flowers and wine. It was great and we advanced a long way without meeting any opposition at all but, in the end, the situation turned sour. We got bogged down deep inside Russia in mid-winter.

I knew that both sides had suffered horrendous hardship and

enormous casualties on the Eastern Front, and I asked him if he was captured. He told me that he was wounded and lost the sight of one eye. Then, after treatment in a field hospital, he was promoted to *feldwebel* and sent back to his unit at the front. Eventually, the military situation became hopeless and the only sensible course was to retreat, but Hitler ordered his army to stand firm and fight to the death. Karl told me:

> We knew it was madness and, if we did not retreat, we would all die. Our officer was a twenty-year-old ardent Nazi. He said we must obey orders; there would be no retreat. The rest of us decided, after a lot of argument among ourselves, that we had no hope of survival unless we shot the officer. We had just agreed which one of us should kill him, when a Russian projectile fatally wounded him and the rest of us escaped.

I realised that it must have been difficult for a group of highly disciplined German troops to agree to kill their officer and I wondered how often other troops had taken the opportunity to kill their superiors during the confusion of battle. I remember how some of us loathed those, whom we regarded as the callous fools of our high command, who manipulated us from far off places of safety. I remember men wryly expressing the wish to drop a bomb on GHQ Cairo. Frustratingly, we never had an opportunity to confront the members of our high command. If we wanted to appeal to higher authorities, we had to address our complaints via our squadron commander, who would be most unlikely to pass them on.

Konrad, another former German soldier, told me:

> Before we left Germany for overseas service, we received our Afrikakorps sleeve insignia and we strutted around, proudly showing off to the girls. The designation 'Afrikakorps' made us feel that we were elite troops and we were excited about seeing such an exotic country as Africa.

Listening to Konrad reminded me how we Royal Air Force lads had felt when we finished training and got our flying badges. We hurried into town to show off to the girls and we admired the reflections of ourselves in shop windows. Some of our young lads rushed off to the photographers and sent photographs home to their parents. We scoffed at the ones who dressed themselves in flying kit for the photographs. In some respects, we had much in common with the young German lads.

After the defeat of the Panzerarmee Afrika in North Africa, Konrad was transferred to the Russian Front, where he was wounded twice, patched up, and sent back into action. When food became scarce, he and his companions were throwing grenades into a lake to stun fish and he was hit by exploding metal fragments. The military authorities assumed that his latest wounds were due to enemy action and, as three times wounded meant repatriation, he was returned to Germany. Later he ended up on the western front where he was taken prisoner by the British. When, in the tranquillity of a peacetime summer afternoon, he proudly showed me photographs of his pretty little granddaughter, I realized that if we had killed him the child and her mother would not have existed. Being able to talk to people like Konrad, with no feeling of animosity on either side, brought home the futility and obscenity of war to me, and generated a constant loathing of those who caused it. In civilized countries, where it is illegal to train dogs to fight each other, men are specially trained to kill people. The purpose of the killing is often obscure or invalid and rarely for true reasons of national security, despite what the warmongers may deceive us into believing at the time.

The war had not been over long when I was chatting with an ex-Luftwaffe pilot. He told me:

> It could easily happen again. All it would take is another strong leader like Hitler and our people would follow him blindly. You see, our people obey every official decree without question. Our problem is the German sense of discipline. For example, if soldiers of various nationalities were ordered to shoot everybody over a certain height, the Russians would go around shooting the biggest people indiscriminately. The British soldiers might question the validity of the order, but ours would painstakingly measure everybody accurately to ensure

that they shot the right ones. Unfortunately, German discipline, blind obedience and the pack instinct are our national characteristics.

I asked him what it was like in his home town at the beginning of the war. I wanted to make a comparison with the atmosphere in Britain. I asked him, 'Were people afraid? After all, it was only just over twenty years since the previous war.' He said:

I remember it was like *Fasching* (carnival time) in the beginning. Some people went wild with excitement. They were like yapping dogs. I was a member of HJ (Hitler Youth Movement). HJ was very popular and we all wanted to be in that. We had uniforms and, at night, we marched through the streets with burning torches. It was good fun and we looked forward to the day when we could join up and see some action.

I don't think he was describing the attitude of the general population, but rather that of his young companions. Hitler's personal interpreter, Dr Paul Schmidt, wrote in his memoirs that when Neville Chamberlain toured Munich after a pre-war meeting with Hitler, people in the street hailed him as 'Chamberlain the peacemaker'. They were obviously not enthusiastic for war. During the few days between Hitler's attack on Poland and Chamberlain's declaration of war, the British Ambassador encountered no sign of hostility from German civilians as he drove through the streets of Berlin in his official car with its Union Jack pennant. Our Ambassador reported that, even after Britain had declared war on them, the German people showed no sign of hostility towards him and his staff. Germans who remembered the carnage of the First World War were alarmed by the prospect of another conflict. One man told him, 'Youth may be enthusiastic for war, but age certainly is not.'

When listening to the ex-Luftwaffe pilot, I realized that my young friends and I had, in some respects, not been much different to the young Germans. A lot of us wanted to be Spitfire pilots, so before the war we joined the Air Defence Cadet Corps. We wore air force blue uniforms, learned Morse code, aircraft recognition, arms drill and other air force related subjects in our spare time. When the war started, we welcomed the opportunity it gave us to join the Royal Air Force and fly aeroplanes. We were aeroplane crazy. We neither knew nor cared about the political situation. We were carried along on a wave of enthusiasm for flying and were unaware of exactly what we were getting ourselves into. The armed forces of all sides were able to rely on a multitude of eager young volunteers like us and, as usual in time of war, the required total number of combatants was reached through massive compulsory conscription of cannon fodder.

I remember how calmly the adult population of Britain reacted to the declaration of war. Hitler, with his comical moustache, was widely regarded with ridicule, as were his henchmen, the fat Göring, the wild-eyed Hess and the evil little propaganda minister Goebbels.

My friend Fred Jobson joined the Royal Air Force in peacetime and, when war became imminent, he was put in charge of a barrage balloon site in a public park and told to get his men to dig a trench. After the trench was completed, an elderly officer (a veteran of the First World War) turned up and said, 'That straight trench is no use. Fill it in and dig a zigzag one instead.' Jobson and his men had just finished digging when the motherly lady from a house bordering the park climbed onto a little wooden box and shouted over the boundary hedge, 'Mr Jobson! The Prime Minister has just been on the wireless. War has been declared. I have put the kettle on. Bring your lads round for a cup of tea.' Her casual reaction to the outbreak of war was typical of the British population's mood at that time. Incidentally, Fred Jobson subsequently volunteered for aircrew service and we trained together at air schools in South Africa. I met him again in Italy where he served as a Navigator on Wellington bombers of Number 70 Squadron.

Most Germans were unwilling to discuss Nazi atrocities with me and many denied knowledge of the death camps, but I knew one man who did not shirk discussion of the Holocaust. I nicknamed him Mr Broadside because one of his favourite expressions in German meant, 'Don't forget the lunch break (Brotzeit).' He had been a chief engineer on the railway in Bavaria and was one of the first people to learn about the death camps. He told me:

Before the war, trains loaded with people were often shunted into the sidings overnight and I was told that the people were criminals in transit to prisons. When I saw that the trains contained old women and young children, I knew they were not criminals. They were various political prisoners and innocent Jewish families, and I thought 'this is all wrong', but I dared not say anything. My assistant was a senior Nazi Party official and if I had protested about the cruel way the people were packed into the trains, he would have caused my family to be locked up with them. I had to consider the safety of my wife and daughter, so I kept my mouth shut, like a lot of other people. I must admit that I really had nothing against Hitler, until I found out about the concentration camps. He gave us full employment and holidays for the first time in our lives. In the beginning, he gave us happiness and national pride. I did not realize that he was actually a lunatic.

Hitler fooled many other people and he even had a number of admirers in Britain before the war. The eminent politician Lloyd George was reported to have publicly expressed his admiration of Hitler after meeting him in Germany. Several prominent members of the British aristocracy, including the Duke of Windsor, shared his favourable opinion of Hitler.

CHAPTER NINE

At the height of the Cold War I frequently travelled to Hungary and Czechoslovakia with my Austrian friend Karl. Driving from Karl's offices in Vienna we could reach Budapest or Prague within a couple of hours. There was very little motor traffic through the Iron Curtain borders in those days and we always followed the same procedure. We called out the sleepy Austrian border guards and took them for a glass of wine in the nearby hostelry where they informed us if any other people had crossed the border recently. In contrast to the Austrian frontiers, comprising simple red and white striped wooden poles, the Iron Curtain crossing places, set back a few hundred yards from the western borders, were formidable steel barriers mounted in concrete supports and manned by armed troops. They were designed to prevent people from escaping to the west, rather than for keeping us out. For years the same officials were in charge of the Czech and Hungarian border posts and that was where we obtained our visas. When the top man opened his desk drawer to take out his visa stamps, we dropped in a couple of chocolate bars and a ball pen. The poorly-paid officials greeted us each time like long lost friends. The welcoming atmosphere at the Czech and Hungarian frontiers at the height of the Cold War might have astonished the people who aimed their NATO weapons at the 'bloody communists'. Another thing that might have surprised people in the 'Free World' was the apparent absence of Soviet troops in most of the Soviet satellite countries.

As soon as we entered Czechoslovakia, we always remarked how much prettier the girls in the villages were than the girls in Vienna but, as very busy businessmen, we had no time to dally with them, of course.

In Budapest we usually stayed in the prestigious Duna or Gellert hotels, but on one occasion both were full up, so we booked into the

Royal and spent the rest of the day visiting the State Trading Enterprises. In the evening we wined and dined our clients at the famous Matyas Pince restaurant and returned to the Royal about midnight. As we entered the hotel we saw people dancing in a room adjoining the lobby and Karl suggested going in for a nightcap. I had travelled from England the previous day and was tired but, at Karl's insistence, I joined him for 'just one cognac'. At my insistence, we sat at a table close to the door, as far away as possible from the band and the tiny dance floor. Mirror panels covered the entire wall of the narrow room and we noticed the reflection of two very elegant women sitting about fifteen feet away from us. One of the women began waving and beckoning us to join them, and Karl said to me, 'She wants to dance with you.' I replied, 'As soon as I finish this drink, I'm off to bed. You dance with her, if you like.' Karl, in mischievous mood, said, 'If you dance with her, I will dance with the other one.' It had become a sort of childish dare. The large amount of wine and *Barack* (apricot spirit) that we had drunk with our clients during the evening made for frivolous behaviour and I said, 'OK, you stand up first.' I suspected that he might clear off to bed as soon as I approached the women, but he assured me, 'Go on, you dance with the one who is waving and I will dance with the other one.' I was surprised that these two expensively dressed women were alone and guessed they must be important western visitors. We walked over to them and as soon as my dance partner stood up, I realised that she was dead drunk. She put her arms around my neck and draped herself on me like a damp cloth. As she tottered to the dance floor, she continually whispered something unintelligible into my ear. Dancing was out of the question and I had difficulty in supporting her. I hoped the music would stop before she fell down. After what seemed like ages, the music paused and I assisted her back to her table where two well-dressed men had appeared. I thanked her and nodded an acknowledgement to the stern-faced men. I said to Karl, 'Come on, let's go.' On our way through the lobby, we went into the toilet. Karl was in high spirits and he began to joke, 'Did you give her your room number? She obviously fancied you. You would be all right there. You should have given her your room number.' I said, 'Don't be silly. She was dead drunk.' He continued to joke about the woman, 'She would sober up eventually. You missed your chance there.' We were both speaking German as Karl did not understand English. Suddenly the door of a cubicle burst open and a balding middle-aged man shrieked in German, '*Hitlerschwein*! How dare you talk like that about my wife?' He continued to rave as he rushed at Karl who grabbed him by the throat with both hands and began choking him. I thought that '*Hitlerschwein*' was a bit too near the truth as Karl had served in the German army. Just as the man appeared to be about to collapse, Karl released him and, coughing, he staggered out of the toilets. There had been a lot of shouting and, as we went out into the lobby, the hotel porter was coming to find out what was going on. I said to him jokingly, 'That man called me a *Hitlerschwein*. He can't say that to me; I am English.' The porter replied, 'He also is English.' I said, 'I can tell by the way he speaks German that he is neither German nor English.' The porter explained, 'He was born here, but he is English now. He is a big man in the film business.' I asked about the women and the other two men, and he said, 'There were three women at first, but they took one away because she was drunk. All the men are in the film business and the women are famous film stars.' We did not see the film people again in Budapest but, about a month later, we were chatting to the director of the Alcron Hotel in Prague when I saw the man whom Karl had half strangled. We were standing by the reception desk in the foyer when the man came in from the street. He took one startled look at us, then turned tail and scuttled out of the hotel. We never saw him again and I regret that we had no opportunity to explain that we meant no harm by our jocular banter about the gorgeous girl who unexpectedly turned out to be his wife.

When travelling with Karl, I often recalled how he said that he and his fellow soldiers had eagerly looked forward to their trip to invade England. Most of them had never travelled far from their home towns until they joined the German Army. Very few of the lads from inland provinces had seen the sea and ships, so the prospect of a boat trip to England seemed to them like a great adventure. Our bombers attacked the barges that were being prepared to convey the invaders to England and our fighter pilots proved to be a match for those of the Luftwaffe, so it is not surprising that Hitler called off the invasion of England. At that time, Britain was not much of a threat to him. Half of our bombs were being dropped in open fields and our army was incapable of invading the continent. An occupation of Britain would have tied down German troops and our poverty-stricken country had no resources worth invading for anyway. We had no oilfields, for instance, whereas the Soviet Union had everything that Germany needed – oilfields, iron ore, vast cornfields and plenty of 'Lebensraum' (living space). Hitler had nothing to gain by an invasion of England. Dr Paul Schmidt, his personal interpreter, reported that, in September 1939, when he informed Hitler that Britain had declared war on Germany, he exclaimed, 'Why have they done that? I have no quarrel with the British Empire.' Apparently he admired the way that little Britain was able to control its vast empire on which it was said 'the sun never sets'. His expressed wish was that while Germany would control the whole of the European continent, the British Empire would act as a stabilizing influence on the rest of the world. Fortunately for us, his attack on Russia proved to be his undoing; it saved us, but it cost the lives of millions.

Hitler was not alone in issuing insane orders like 'no surrender, no retreat' and 'fight to the death', but not every commander complied with such idiotic instructions. Field Marshal Paulus sensibly defied Hitler and surrendered his beaten army at Stalingrad after many months of savage fighting.

The British prime minister also gave a similar order in February 1942 when Lieutenant General Arthur Percival was in command on Singapore Island. Churchill ordered that the island was to be defended at all costs and officers were to fight to the death alongside their troops. He was incensed when the island fell to the Japanese. Large numbers of captured personnel died a slow death at the hands of the Japanese who, in accordance with their warrior code, despised all prisoners of war. British servicemen who managed to survive Japanese imprisonment, sickness, cruelty and neglect faced years of post-war battles for help from their own callous government.

After the war I built up a very profitable business relationship with clients in Japan. As a wartime flyer, I wanted to add to my knowledge about the kamikaze suicide pilots, but I found that most Japanese were reluctant to discuss the war; they had obviously had enough. During the first of many business visits, I toured the country with my Japanese agent, Sota San. One evening, as we dined in a hotel restaurant, Sota showed me photographs of himself in military uniform and I asked him where they were taken. He told me that he had been fighting in Manchuria and I started, tactfully, to probe for information about the war from the Japanese perspective.

I mentioned the matter of Japanese brutality to prisoners of war. Sota told me, 'The prisoners were not the only ones who suffered. Our authorities also treated our own Japanese soldiers harshly and we were half starved most of the time.' I said, 'Surely there is no excuse for the exceptionally cruel way the thousands of prisoners taken at Singapore were treated.' Sota's reply gave me an understanding of the Japanese mentality. 'In Japan there is no respect for soldiers who surrender. Our Japanese soldiers never surrender. We regarded those soldiers as cowards.'[1]

There seemed no point in continuing the discussion, and I seldom mentioned the war to him again. The talk of 'no surrender' reminded me that we bomber crews were ordered not to turn back when our aircraft were damaged by enemy action. We were to press on to our target, despite the likelihood that the plane, with its fragile stressed-skin construction, might break up in the air. Turning back was regarded as cowardice and the safety of airmen was not to be considered until after we had dropped our bombs. However, these callous orders were disregarded by us when wounded men were on board.

While working in Japan, I never succeeded in learning much more than I already knew about the wartime kamikaze pilots. I understood that any men who did not deliberately crash onto their targets were condemned to death for cowardice. The post-war

Japanese taxi drivers, who drove everywhere at a terrifying speed, laughingly referred to themselves as kamikaze, but nobody else mentioned the word to me.

As a former participant in our strategic bomber offensive, I was curious about the Japanese post-war reaction to the dropping of the two atomic bombs, but I never heard anyone mention that dreadful matter. However, I was enjoying an evening out with my Japanese business partners when we called at a bar with a dance band and a few unattached young women. My friends took dance partners and I followed suit. I chose a girl who was unusually tall and, finding that she spoke a little English, I asked her where she was from. She answered, 'Nagasaki.' My first reaction was to wonder if she was radioactive, but then I realized that she could not have been there when the bomb was dropped. I felt uneasy about the thought that some of her relatives might have been victims of the bomb and I was very glad that I had no part in it.

Publisher's note:

1 The Japanese treatment of prisoners of war during the Second World War was in contrast to their adherence to international conventions on prisoners in both the First World War and the Russo-Japanese War. The brutality in the Second World War appears to have been a decision of the military faction of the Japanese government.

CHAPTER TEN

Despite its status as a Soviet satellite state, Hungary was a delightful country with its excellent food, wine, gypsy music, friendly people and an engineering industry that needed my machinery and technology. Disastrously, the people of Budapest rose up against their communist oppressors in 1956 and the Red Army swiftly sent tanks to quell the insurrection. The hapless people of Budapest could expect no sign of concern from the British government. It was far too preoccupied at the time with a disastrous attempt to stop Egypt from nationalizing the Suez Canal. While British soldiers fought the Egyptians, the United States government expressed its strong disapproval of the ill-fated British adventure and, typically, our government awarded no medals to the British soldiers who participated in the Suez fiasco. During my visits to Hungary shortly after the failed uprising, I noticed an increased anti-Russian feeling and a strong yearning for freedom. I thought it would be a long time before any of the Kremlin's other satellites dared to challenge their masters after the brutal suppression of the Hungarians' attempt became known.

My commercial activity was unaffected by fluctuations in the East/West political situation, but I felt uneasy when I was behind the Iron Curtain on occasions when the nuclear powers were engaged in tit-for-tat expulsions of diplomats and spies. I hoped the clowns in their nuclear bunkers would not press the button while I was in the target area.

Aitch was the fifty-year-old managing director of one of my British suppliers. During the war, he had served as a senior naval officer on the administrative staff of the Admiralty. One day he asked me to take him with me on a trip to Hungary. Hoping that he would not be too much of a nuisance, I agreed. He seemed to think that Budapest's nightlife would be like that of Paris and we had no sooner arrived than he pestered me to take him to a night club. I explained that there were no night clubs behind the Iron Curtain and I took him to a performance at the State Opera House instead.

My main contact in Budapest was Madame Fischer, the clever head of the relevant state purchasing department, and Aitch was keen to meet her. I can only describe that lady as a true vamp, an unscrupulous flirt, who seemed to have stepped straight out of an old black-and-white spy movie. She was charming. She was elegant and she spoke at least half a dozen languages. Her persuasive tactics were always distracting during negotiations over price discounts. Instead of discussing new business with me as planned, she immediately pounced on Aitch. Sitting on a low chair and displaying her long legs, she leaned towards him with her elbow on her knee and slowly eased her skirt back to reveal a little more thigh. I had recently finalized a contract with Madam Fischer and ordered machinery from Aitch's factory. Foolishly, he mentioned it to her. It is a golden rule in our business that once a sale has been agreed, the vendor should stop talking about it. Madam Fischer quickly realized that she had an easy victim. Fluttering her mascara-coated eyelashes, and slowly puffing smoke through a long cigarette holder, she appealed in her husky Hungarian accent for an extra discount. Aitch soon began to look flustered and after about half an hour she had wrung an extra two per cent discount out of him. As we left the building, he asked me, 'Well, how did I do?'

I told him, 'I had already sent my contract to your firm about ten days ago, so you did not need to give a discount, but as you did, it will have to come out of your company's funds, not mine.'

He blurted irritably, 'It's your bloody fault. You did not let me get near a woman all the week and now you confronted me with that blasted creature.'

I laughed at him. Nothing during his time at the Admiralty or later had prepared him for an encounter with the formidable Madam Fischer. He never suggested making another overseas trip with me.

Apart from Aitch, and members of my family, I rarely

encountered navy personnel. My younger brother left home at the age of fifteen, lied about his age and served as a wartime telegraphist/air gunner in the Fleet Air Arm. Our uncle left his job as a senior executive of a large grocery chain, joined the Navy as an ordinary seaman and swiftly rose to the rank of lieutenant commander. After the war, my brother had difficulty in settling down to civilian life. Following his release from the Navy, he joined the Royal Air Force and served for a short time before moving to Australia and joining the army. The last time we met in Australia he had just returned from a spell of combat duty in Vietnam. I think his war service had made him a bit crazy. A lot of us were the same.

My pal Robin Black was typical of many ex-Bomber Command men who, although never injured physically, suffered the dire long-term effects of too much stress. He lost his job as a senior representative of an engineering company after he abandoned an important foreign client to fend for himself during a drunken night out in London. His hitherto tolerant boss finally decided to sack him after he crashed two company cars into trees and abandoned them at the scene. When he could no longer afford the rent of his London apartment, or the cost of moving his things out, I offered my help. I gathered up armfuls of his clothes and carried them out to my car for the journey to a dingy single basement room that was to be his new accommodation. As I carefully placed his air force tunic on the back seat of my car, I noticed his flying badge and ribbon of the Distinguished Flying Cross. Robin was one of the many forgotten victims of war who would never be able to settle down after the psychological trauma of air combat. Later, I discovered that he lay in a diabetic coma for four days in his basement room before being discovered and carted off to the local hospital's intensive care ward.

In a street market I met a German who had served in submarines during the war. His wartime base was on the coast of France and I joked that he and his young pals must have had fun with the French girls.

He said, 'We did not often see any.'

I asked, 'What about shore leave?'

He answered, 'We had to stay at sea until we had sunk a specified tonnage of ships, so we rarely had any shore leave.'

I knew about the enormous losses of German submarines and said that I would not have wanted to serve in submarines. He said:

Admittedly, we had a dangerous job, but I admire you flying men. I am terrified of heights, you see, and I don't even like to go up ladders. Before I joined the Kriegsmarine, I worked in a factory and one morning I came home after working on the night shift, and my mother told me to go up and clear the guttering. I climbed up a ladder with a bucket and a trowel, but when I got to the top I could not let go of the ladder to take the trowel out of the bucket. I could not even come down. I just stood there petrified. People passing in the street shouted good morning to me, but I dared not look down. After a while, my mother came out of the house and asked me why I was taking so long. I asked her to tell my neighbour that I wanted to have a word with him. When he arrived, I asked him to come up the ladder behind me and take the bucket so I could come down holding on with both hands. As I said, I really do admire you flying men. I could not do your job, high up in the air.

I did not tell him that we seldom felt any sensation of height when flying.

One of my post-war acquaintances, 'German George', was a seventeen-year-old Bavarian farm boy who had never seen the sea until he was drafted into the German submarine service. His base was in the south of France where I dropped thousands of leaflets exhorting the Germans to surrender to our invading troops. I had always regarded leaflet dropping as a dangerous waste of effort. I asked George how he and his fellow sailors reacted to the leaflets. He said:

They were very useful and we were glad to have them. When there were no more on the ground, we climbed up into the trees to collect them. In 1944 we had not a scrap of toilet paper, so we were very grateful to the Royal Air Force for sending us some.

I doubt if many Germans used the leaflets for their intended purpose. Inevitably, some of our planes were shot down while delivering the blasted leaflets. Incidentally, the Royal Air Force called the leaflets 'Nickels'. I wondered why they were so fond of using silly code words. The foil strips that we dropped to upset enemy radar were officially called 'Window' and the dropping of mines was called 'gardening'. Our mines were dropped in specified 'beds' in the Danube. I never understood why certain things were not called by their proper names, although bombs, pyrotechnics and targets were. I pictured a multitude of earthbound 'penguins' at the Air Ministry in London busily thinking up silly ideas for no apparent purpose.

Bedrich, my language tutor, fled from his home in Vienna when the German troops arrived. He told me:

> Although I wanted to support Britain's fight against the Nazis, I did not want to kill anyone. To prove that I was not a coward, I decided to do something really dangerous without actually fighting.

His opportunity came when he saw a Norwegian Merchant Navy appeal for recruits in the *London Times* newspaper. He signed on as an engine-room greaser on a Norwegian oil tanker, thinking that was a suitably hazardous non-combatant job at a time when shipping losses were high. The greatest danger to merchant ships came from German submarines and one of them torpedoed the oil tanker. The tanker's crew took to the life rafts and the submarine's crew picked up the survivors. The German captain asked for personal details from each of the tanker's crew and when it came to Bedrich's turn, he blurted out, 'I am not Norwegian, I am Austrian.' As Austria was united with Germany, he fully expected to be shot as a traitor on the spot. The captain ignored the outburst and casually started dealing with the next man. Bedrich's frantic cry, 'Not only am I Austrian, I am also a Jew', made no impression whatsoever on the captain. The tanker's crew members, including Bedrich, were put ashore on enemy-occupied territory and interned until the end of the war.

After the war Bedrich was engaged as the leader of a team of interpreters at the Hamburg and Nuremberg War Crimes trials, where the victors made up the rules and decided who should live and who should die. Bedrich told me, 'In my opinion, some of the German military officers should not have been charged. They were not all Nazi criminals.' No doubt he remembered the German submarine commander who clearly did not follow Hitler's obsessive doctrine of anti-Semitism.

Throughout the war, the western Allies unwisely disregarded the growing anti-Hitler movement within the German military establishment. The British and American authorities gave no encouragement to the German officers who risked their lives in attempts to overthrow the Nazi regime. The Germans made at least four failed attempts to kill Hitler during the war. The last assassination attempt in July 1944 came nearest to success and the German officers who supported it paid with their lives. Instead of encouraging the plotters, the Allies persisted in calling for German unconditional surrender, and thousands more innocent women and children died on both sides while the European war dragged on for another year. Perhaps the German civilians cowering in their bunkers during the devastating Allied air raids might have reflected on Prime Minister Chamberlain's radio broadcast to them on the day after the British declaration of war. He said:

> In this war we are not fighting against you, the German people, for whom we have no bitter feeling, but against your tyrannous regime, which has betrayed not only its own people, but the whole of Western civilization and all that you and we hold dear. May God defend the right!

Our war leaders later disregarded the fact that our true enemy was the evil Nazi regime, not the civilian population. Instead of giving moral or material support to the German opponents of the Nazi regime, we continued punishing the German population at large while needlessly sacrificing more of our own troops. There was no sense in continuing to slaughter the wives and families of German combatants who obeyed their masters just as we obeyed ours. The German people were to become our Cold War allies and a tremendous drain on our financial resources as soon as the war ended, so why did we not encourage them in their wartime efforts to oppose Hitler?

Unfortunately, our war leaders seemed blind to the fact that the opposition movement within Germany was our strongest potential ally. Perhaps our leaders were too preoccupied with quarrelling amongst themselves to think about the most obvious, quickest and cheapest way to end the slaughter.

As soon as the war ended, the victorious Allies scrambled to outbid each other in attempts to recruit all the clever German scientists and industrialists, regardless of the fact that many had been ardent supporters of the Nazi regime.

Throughout the war, our ally Stalin was presented to the British public as benign 'Uncle Joe', although he was actually a lifelong mass murderer. One of Stalin's many heinous crimes was the slaughter in 1940 of over 4,500 Polish officers in a forest at Katyn near Smolensk. Over the years, other authors have written extensively on the subject of the Katyn massacre, so I only deal here with the way the aftermath of that atrocity affected me and my air force friends during the 1944 Warsaw Uprising. At the time we could not understand why our Russian allies fired on us while we conveyed supplies of arms and ammunition to Warsaw's beleaguered Poles. We did not know why Stalin would not permit us to land on airfields situated only twenty minutes flying time from Warsaw, thereby forcing us to make hazardous round trips of about 1,800 miles from our bases in Italy. We did not know why we were given the difficult and dangerous task of supporting the distant uprising when the Red Army was already encamped in Warsaw's outskirts. We airmen knew nothing about the political circumstances. Our dead friends will never know the truth, but those of us who survived to learn the facts will never forget how Stalin's dispute with the Poles cost the lives of our airmen.

The Polish government in exile in London correctly accused the Soviet government of the 1940 Katyn massacre, but Stalin blamed the Germans although they could not possibly have committed the crime because they did not arrive in the Katyn area until 1943. The date of the massacre was verified from diaries, letters, newspapers and other documents found in the pockets of the Polish corpses. In the ensuing row, Stalin withdrew diplomatic recognition of the

American built Liberator bomber of the RAF. © *AUTHOR'S OWN COLLECTION*.

B24 Liberator bomber of RAF 178 Squadron, en-route to a target in Yugoslavia (photo taken from the author's plane). © *AUTHOR'S OWN COLLECTION*.

Halifax dropping arms to partisans in the Balkans. © *Author's own collection*.

Halifax of 148 Squadron loaded with parachute containers of supplies for the underground resistance fighters. © *Author's own collection*.

Polish General Skalski during his time
in the Royal Air Force.
© AUTHOR'S OWN COLLECTION.

Polish pilot Tomi Tomiczek.
© AUTHOR'S OWN COLLECTION.

German pilot of Molders' Squadron (photo given by him to the author).
© AUTHOR'S OWN COLLECTION.

Polish underground army soldiers. © AUTHOR'S OWN COLLECTION.

Polish partisans in the Krakow area. © AUTHOR'S OWN COLLECTION.

Partisans in the Balkans collecting air-dropped supplies. © *Author's own collection*.

Partisans at the Drop Zone during a supply drop. © *Author's own collection*.

RAF Pilot Officer Coates of 31 SAAF Squadron resting next to his RAF Liberator bomber. © *AUTHOR'S OWN COLLECTION.*

Twenty-two year old Ken Trevenor, Flight Commander of 178 Squadron with crew members. © *AUTHOR'S OWN COLLECTION.*

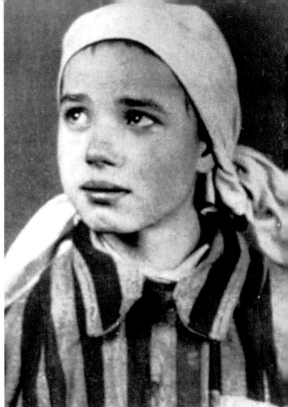

Woman soldier of the Polish Armia Krajowa. © *AUTHOR'S OWN COLLECTION*.

Thirteen year old political prisoner of Auschwitz who died a few months after capture (photo taken from the Auschwitz Archives). © *AUTHOR'S OWN COLLECTION*.

A group of Polish underground resistance soldiers. © *AUTHOR'S OWN COLLECTION*.

Halifax dropping supplies to partisans in enemy occupied territory from a height of 600ft in daylight. © *Author's own collection.*

A flak-damaged Halifax, crash landed at Brindisi. © *Author's own collection.*

General Borkomorowski, AK Commander in Poland. © *AUTHOR'S OWN COLLECTION*.

Group Captain Ron Hockey, Commander of 161 and 138 Secret SD Squadrons. © *AUTHOR'S OWN COLLECTION*.

Shot-down Canadians under the care of Polish partisans. © *AUTHOR'S OWN COLLECTION*.

King George VI visiting his troops. © AUTHOR'S OWN COLLECTION.

Crew of 178 Squadron with their giant Liberator bomber. © AUTHOR'S OWN COLLECTION.

148 Squadron men dropping supplies to partisans from a Halifax.
© AUTHOR'S OWN COLLECTION.

The RAF shadowing a Russian plane en-route to Cuba. © AUTHOR'S OWN COLLECTION.

Winston Churchill visiting his troops.
© AUTHOR'S OWN COLLECTION.

Duke of Gloucester visiting an American Air Base. His Czech pilot stands on the far left. The plane is a DC3 Dakota.
© AUTHOR'S OWN COLLECTION.

im Auton with Polish Ambassador Professor Gertych (an ex-partisan at the BBMF during the Cold War), the Polish Consul General and Defence Attache. © *AUTHOR'S OWN COLLECTION*.

Author's snapshot of Polish President General Jaruselski visiting Polish graves at Newark-on-Trent. © *AUTHOR'S OWN COLLECTION*.

War cemetery at Krakow in Poland, containing graves of airmen killed while supporting the Poles during the 1944 uprising. © *Author's own collection*.

Hungary. Graves of airmen shot down en-route to or from Warsaw during the 1944 uprising. © *Author's own collection*.

Memorial to 50 people shot down in a Warsaw street as reprisal for anti-Nazi action by the Polish Secret Resistance Forces. © *AUTHOR'S OWN COLLECTION.*

The crypt where the Czech parachutists where holed-up after assassinating Heydrich. © *AUTHOR'S OWN COLLECTION.*

The author with Czech Ministry of Defence officials reviewing troops in Prague.
© *AUTHOR'S OWN COLLECTION*.

The author helping Rumanian Air Force veterans to repair war graves in Hungary.
© *AUTHOR'S OWN COLLECTION*.

Polish government in London and later opposed our flights to aid Warsaw's Poles. We lost 90 per cent of the planes that attempted to reach Warsaw and many of our casualties resulted directly from Stalin's dispute with the Polish government in exile. To their eternal shame, the British government sided with Stalin and asserted that the Germans were responsible for the massacre, despite abundant evidence to the contrary. When the Poles persisted in blaming Stalin, they were told to stop 'rocking the boat'. As usual, Stalin had to be appeased at all costs.

After the war the British authorities even opposed the erection by the émigré Poles of a Katyn memorial in London because it was to bear the true date of the massacre. However, in 1989, President Gorbachev of the Soviet Union confirmed that the Poles were right. He disclosed that Stalin had personally ordered the murder of the Polish officers at Katyn in 1940. In fact, Stalin gave instructions that 25,000 Poles of the officer class were to be shot. As mentioned earlier, my Polish Air Force friend Jozef Polilejko was spared the fate of the officers because he was just a lowly corporal pilot. Stalin was intent on eliminating the Polish officer class just as he had purged his own military establishment.

In recent years the British government has expressed regret for past crimes such as the slave trade, although there are no people alive who were involved in it. In view of Gorbachev's disclosure of Stalin's responsibility for the Katyn murders, an apology is surely overdue to the Polish people for Britain's disgraceful attitude to them when evidence of the Katyn massacre was first discovered.

During the Cold War I often accompanied Polish Air Force veterans on visits to Warsaw's cemetery where the communist government had situated a large horizontal Katyn memorial slab bearing the wrong date. In customary Polish manner, the population regularly placed lighted candles on the memorial. I noticed that the candles were deliberately positioned so that an accumulation of candle wax permanently masked the false date.

After the fall of communism the Poles opened a Katyn memorial museum in Warsaw. It contains such exhibits as military badges, buttons, diaries and other personal possessions found on the exhumed corpses at Katyn. The sad sight of tearful visiting relatives of the murdered men adds to the sombre atmosphere of the place.

While we in Italy were making desperate attempts to support the beleaguered Poles in Warsaw by dropping our inadequate loads of guns and ammunition, Polish troops under British command were participating in Operation MARKET GARDEN – the largest and most disastrous airborne action of the war. The operation was undertaken despite evidence from the RAF's aerial reconnaissance photographs that the remnants of two German panzer divisions were deployed in the Arnhem area[1], and warnings from Bletchley Park's code-breakers on the presence of German troops.

The Dutch resistance organization had warned the Allies about the presence of German troops near Arnhem, but this information was disregarded as the Germans were known to have penetrated the Dutch resistance. This brings me to another huge blunder. My friends of Tempsford's Number 138 (Special Duties) Squadron dropped scores of secret agents and radio operators into enemy-occupied territory to work with local resistance groups.

One of these agents, parachuted into Holland, was captured by the Germans and forced to send false radio messages to London, as though he was working with the resistance. In accordance with the standard Special Operations Executive (SOE) procedures, he warned the Dutch section of SOE in London that he had been captured. He did so by making an agreed secret indication in his radio messages, but the people in London ignored the warning, although he repeated it in every message. Using the captured radio operator, the Germans were able to arrange for further agents and large quantities of equipment to be delivered into their hands.

Eventually the Germans had obtained so much equipment from London that they had to find additional local warehouse storage space. The captured British agents were tortured and either shot or imprisoned. This affair, called by the Germans the 'Englandspiel' (England game), was one of many blunders in which my RAF friends were involved unwittingly. It was another shocking waste of air force effort, vital war material and British agents.[2]

When weather conditions permitted, I preferred to drive to my business destinations behind the Iron Curtain instead of flying. The use of the car allowed me to make regular visits to engineering factories and familiarise the production directors with the latest western manufacturing technology and machinery. The directors could then use the exact specifications of my particular products when sending requests for quotations through their state trading corporations. Consequently, my offers were the only ones that corresponded exactly with the client's demands. Wining and dining of clients was customary behind the Iron Curtain, just as in the west. The tactful use of various inducements or 'sweeteners' greatly facilitated business transactions; but when vendors applied corrupt practices carelessly, imprisonment of both parties resulted. Apart from the obvious dangers, business behind the Iron Curtain was beset with hidden pitfalls to trap the unwary visitor. The prohibited photographing of anything owned by the state made the use of a camera inadvisable in countries where the state owned everything. The ban on photography applied to such things as planes, trains, railway stations, bridges, post offices, police officers, soldiers and military installations. In other words, cameras were banned everywhere and I never saw a local person with one.

Surprisingly, I was completely free to drive around unhindered in the Soviet satellite countries. I was supposed to obtain prior permission from the Ministry of the Interior before visiting factories but I never complied with that tedious formality. When travelling by car, I carefully avoided anything resembling a military installation and, during over thirty years of Iron Curtain visits, I only felt in danger from the military authorities on one occasion.

Driving at night behind the Iron Curtain was a dangerous undertaking. Town streets were dimly lit and country roads were in total darkness. There were no white lines on the rough road surfaces. Reflective 'cat's-eyes' were unknown and hazard warning signs were rare. Motor traffic was scarce, but in villages horse-drawn farm carts without lights were a frequent danger after dark.

One damp evening in the early 1960s, I drove alone towards the Czech town of Hradec Kralove when, in pitch darkness, my three-month-old Rover car broke down. After several unsuccessful attempts to get going, I got out of the car and peered around in the darkness. I found that I was stranded next to a concrete bunker, directly opposite the gates of an army camp. That was just about the worst place to be broken down in the middle of the Cold War. There was a rather bored-looking armed sentry at the gates and I went across the road to ask him, in my version of the Czech language, if there was a transport section in the camp. I was hoping that I might be able to get help from an army mechanic in exchange for a bribe. No such luck. The sentry shrugged his shoulders and then turned away and ignored me. I went back and sat in the car while I considered my predicament.

A few minutes later, I saw a civilian approaching out of the darkness. I got out of the car to ask him if there was a garage nearby where I might find a mechanic. I was glad to discover that he was a Slovak because I understood the Slovak language better than I understood Czech. He asked me for a pencil and paper and started to draw a street map. When I saw that he had written the words military barracks and bunker on the drawing, I stopped him. A sketch of that sort could land me in jail. I asked him to wait a minute while I again attempted to drive the car. The engine started, but the car would not move. I thought that perhaps the clutch fluid had leaked out. I was wearing a white shirt and a lightweight Dacron suit and I did not want to get wet and dirty because I was due to meet an important client the next day.

I gave the Slovak some money and asked him to go to the garage and fetch some clutch fluid for me. Obligingly, he agreed and set off into the darkness. I sat in the car and hoped to see him again. When, to my relief, he did return, I saw that he had brought a can of brake fluid and I thought that might be good enough. I located the appropriate filler cap and asked my new friend to look under the car and tell me if the fluid ran out as I poured it in. I gave him a towel to kneel on and, to my surprise, he took off his coat and trousers and, clad in a shirt and colourful striped underpants, crawled under the car. When he reappeared, he assured me that the fluid had not leaked out. Just as he was putting his trousers on, the armed sentry appeared at my side and I noticed that for some reason he had a rifle round dangling on a thin chain from the top button of his tunic. After walking around the car twice, he turned towards us and snarled, 'Imperialists'.

At that moment, an army officer arrived with a uniformed policeman who demanded my passport and immediately stuffed it into his pocket. I was making an unofficial visit to a state-owned factory without bothering to secure prior permission from either the Ministry of the Interior or the state trading organization, so I knew that I would be in trouble if asked to disclose my destination. I was becoming cold and wet, so I got back into the car and awaited further developments. I invited the Slovak to join me and offered him a cigarette. I had already been stuck there for a couple of hours and I hoped I would not be detained for the rest of the night. Neither the army officer nor the policeman spoke English and, surprisingly, they said nothing to the Slovak. The policeman did not seem to know what to do next. He walked around the car a few times, wrote down the registration number, exchanged some words with the army officer, then unexpectedly returned my passport and indicated that I was free to depart. I started the engine and said to the Slovak, 'If the car functions now, I will take you home.' I felt like setting fire to the thing if it did not work.

I drove away and, fortunately, everything seemed to be in order. The Slovak directed me to the place where he lived. I then thanked him and gave him a fistful of Czech money and a pack of 200 American cigarettes. As I resumed my journey to Hradec Kralove, I planned what I would say to the Rover agents in London who had checked the car a few days before I left England. Although this was the only occasion when I feared that I might be in very serious trouble with the military authorities, it was not the only time that I had reason to curse that car.

A couple of weeks later, I was in Moravia when the engine would not start. I sent for a local mechanic who failed to fix it, so I asked him to tow the car as far as the Czech/Austrian border where I would seek help from the Austrian breakdown service. The next day he turned up in a huge Russian car with a solid tow-bar. He hitched my car up and set off at breakneck speed through sleepy villages where we scattered dozens of squawking chickens and I fought with the steering wheel to prevent my car from overturning on the bends. At the Czech frontier the mechanic uncoupled the car and I went into the customs office for a chat with the top man, whom I had known for several years. I explained that my car had conked out and said, 'Can you get some of your men to push it across from here to the Austrian Border?' He told me that such a thing was completely out of the question. I produced a wad of Czech money as an inducement, but he was adamant. He told me, 'If I let my men out through our barrier, they would never come back. I'm very sorry, but I can't help you.' I knew that the Austrians, about a quarter of a mile away, could not come to my assistance, because the barren area of land between the two borders was Czech territory. I fetched some bottles of cola from the car and sat chatting to the border guards. They told me that I was the only traveller to arrive at the border since early the previous day. There were no other buildings nearby and no public telephone facilities. It looked as though I might be stranded there for a long time. Luckily, about an hour later, another car arrived and, while the border guards were searching that car, I explained my predicament to the driver. Fortunately, he was on his way to Austria and he kindly agreed to drive slowly behind my car and push it to the Austrian border.

At the border, I phoned the local breakdown service and, half an hour later, a red-faced man arrived in a little yellow van. He had been celebrating at the local village's annual wine festival and I doubted if he would be of much help. He staggered over to my car and said, 'Start the engine.' I began to explain that a Czech mechanic had spent hours trying in vain to start it. He was not listening. He asked, 'Where's the key?' It was in the ignition. He got into the car and turned the key. The engine started immediately. He drove back and forth a couple of times, got out of the car, shook his head and said, 'There is nothing wrong with that car!' I was lost for words. Apparently, the car had cured itself and made me look a fool. I paid the man for his wasted journey and he departed, still shaking his head. I guessed he would return to the wine festival and laugh with his friends about the daft Englishman who could not start his own car.

As I drove the car all the way back to London without any further trouble, I remembered that we had aeroplanes like that during the war. Sometimes, during night raids, the guns would not fire, automatic cameras, autopilots and other instruments stopped working, and bombs hung up, although everything had worked perfectly during air tests in daylight. On one occasion, the illuminated graticule of the bomb-sight suddenly went blank on the run-up to the target, so I dropped the bombs by guesswork. The target was a railway marshalling yard about five miles long and over a mile wide so, even without a bomb-sight, I could not miss it. It seemed that mythical creatures, that we called gremlins, infected the equipment in some of our clapped-out aeroplanes, but I never expected to encounter gremlins in an expensive modern car. Incidentally, gremlins are still around, and nowadays they lurk mostly in computers and other high tech equipment.

Publisher's note:

1 The remnants of II SS Panzer Corps' divisions, 2nd *Das Reich* and 9th *Hohenstaufen*, had been sent to the area to be re-equipped and reform having been all but destroyed in Normandy. The corps could hardly muster the strength of a brigade, let alone a division, but the few armoured vehicles their battle-groups possessed gave them an advantage over the light troops of 1st Airborne Division.

2 The *Englandspiel* or *Unternehmen Nordpol* – Operation NORTH POLE – eventually resulted in the deaths of fifty-four Dutch, not British, SOE agents, who are commemorated by the Englandspiel, or Fall of Icarus, Monument in The Hague. SOE radio procedures called for security checks to be included in messages. There was no single agent who was sending messages. Although SOE's head of codes, Leo Marks, suspected that something was amiss, it was not until April 1944 that the dropping of agents was stopped.

CHAPTER ELEVEN

As a fluent speaker of Russian I was keen to meet some Russians, but they were surprisingly absent from the satellite countries that they controlled. My opportunity finally came when I visited an exhibition of machinery at the Leipzig Spring Fair in East Germany. At that time the whole of Berlin was like an island in Soviet-occupied East Germany. After flying from London to West Berlin, I booked into the Hotel am Zoo that was situated near the city's *Zoo Bahnhof*. At that time, Berlin comprised sectors that were each administered by the individual Allied powers. Surprisingly, before the erection of the Berlin Wall, people living in the Soviet-controlled sector of East Berlin were at liberty to cross unhindered into the western sectors where their 'Eastmarks' received parity with 'Westmarks', although they were officially of no legal worth outside Soviet-controlled territory. Having learned from West Berliners that travellers from West Berlin into East Germany were locally able to convert Westmarks into Eastmarks at the rate of four to one, I joined the queue at the money exchange booth in the Zoo railway station. It was illegal to take Eastmarks out of Berlin, but who cared? While I waited in the queue, black market moneychangers offered me a better deal than the exchange booth's rate of four to one. By the time I boarded the train for Leipzig, my trouser pockets were so stuffed with wads of Eastmark notes that sitting down was difficult, so I stood in the corridor until the travelling customs officer had completed his rounds. Customs checks on trains were not as strict as at airports and the East German officials, being well aware of the availability of black market currency in West Berlin, probably assumed that nobody would be silly enough to change Westmarks into Eastmarks at the official rate of one to one. There were no body searches and the customs officials went away happily with the gift of a ball pen and a couple of Westmarks in payment for a visa. I did not know what to expect in the Russian-controlled DDR (German Democratic Republic). I knew only that the Russian occupiers had taken away huge quantities of manufacturing plant as reparations and other plunder as the spoils of war.

It was dusk when I alighted from the train in Leipzig's dilapidated railway station. I saw half a dozen young policemen standing on a high gantry. They were dressed in sinister black uniforms, jackboots and black leather helmets. Each grim-faced youth had a machine pistol pointing towards the passengers. The menacing atmosphere could not have been more depressing if the Nazis had still been in control. Not wanting to queue for a taxi, I walked through the dimly lit streets to the state tourist bureau and requested details of accommodation. I was told that there was only one hotel and that was reserved for visiting government delegates. All the other hotels had been destroyed and no new ones had yet been built, but I could have accommodation with a family in a private apartment. There being no alternative, I accepted the situation and made my way to the nearest taxi rank. I showed the driver the address that the tourist office had given me. We set off and he stopped at nearly every street corner to ask the way. He told me that he had been drafted in from his home town of Halle and this was his first time in Leipzig.

Although there was a cold March wind blowing, I noticed that nobody wore scarves or gloves and the women had no handbags. The dim street lamps and ruined buildings created an atmosphere of gloom, and the few people on the streets looked miserable and shabby. It was in stark contrast to West Germany where the people were cosseted by the western Allies. There were no private cars on the streets of Leipzig, but overloaded trams driven by young women raced through the streets with bells clanging. I wondered where the occupying troops of the victorious Red Army were. I had expected to see swarms of them, but I saw none. I was rather surprised and disappointed by their absence; I was, after all, on Stalin's side of the notorious Iron Curtain and I was keen to speak Russian.

On the day after my arrival in Leipzig, I went to the International Exhibition and looked around the various national pavilions. Most exhibitors were from Russia, the Soviet satellite countries and other communist states. A few exhibitors from the West displayed prototypes of machines that seemed to be present merely for propaganda purposes. In their national pavilion, the Russians proudly exhibited their unmanned Sputnik that would be superseded by another one carrying a poor little dog to its death in space. I bought a catalogue and was surprised to see a list of East German factories with their addresses and product details. As a former air bomber, I had expected the locations of such potential targets to be secret, but obviously the communists did not allow the Cold War to hinder the process of international trade.

I parked myself on the stand of a machinery company and learned that the commercial manager had failed to turn up. The engineering staff, having no sales experience and unable to speak foreign languages, were in difficulties, so I stayed to help them. A couple of days later, I was delighted when several Russian army and air force officers appeared on the stand. They all wore smart uniforms with top quality greatcoats and smelled of the same perfume. This was my first meeting with citizens of modern Russia and I had never expected to encounter military personnel. I gathered up some advertising gifts of pocketknives, ball pens and playing cards bearing a company logo, and handed them over to the officers. None of them understood English and I was the first Russian-speaking Englishman they had met. To my delight we were able to laugh and joke like old friends. I teasingly asked, 'What are you going to give me as a souvenir?' One of them suggested a brass button bearing the hammer and sickle, and started to twist it off his greatcoat. Another offered me a collar badge. I protested that I was only joking and I did not want them to vandalize their uniforms. Finally, an officer took me quietly to one side and said, 'Tomorrow I will come back and bring you a very good Russian souvenir.' True to his word, he appeared the following morning with an official lapel badge of the communist Leninist Youth Organization. The inscription on the back showed that it was manufactured at the State Mint. I knew that such badges would only be available to members of the communist organization and it was certainly a most unusual souvenir to be in the possession of an English capitalist like me. In conversation with a local German civilian, I expressed surprise that the Russian officers were so amiable. He replied, Of course they were friendly with you. Nobody else would give anything to those people.' He went on to explain bitterly that when the first Russian troops entered Germany, they terrorized the population and raped hundreds of women and girls.

I could very well understand that some Russian soldiers would exact revenge for similar atrocities committed by the Germans in Russia. However, 'two wrongs don't make a right', as the saying goes. I changed the subject and remarked, 'I am surprised that there are plenty of officers, but no ordinary Russian soldiers in the town.' He replied, 'They have been moved out into the countryside. When they were here, many of them were thrown into the cells overnight by their police patrols and flogged for drunkenness on the streets.' During the war the bravery of the Red Army's ordinary soldiers was legendary and I hoped to meet some of those veterans one day. Of interest to me was the fact that, unlike our air force, the Russian air force had female combatant pilots during the war. I was keen to meet some of those brave women, but I saw no Russian females in Leipzig.

One afternoon I chanced to meet the visiting West German sales agent for a British firm, and he invited me to accompany him on a visit to a Leipzig pub and see what life was like for the local people. We chose a beer cellar where people were dancing to the music of a typical German brass band. As the evening progressed the band started to play western-style dance music and some young couples began to imitate American jive. Suddenly the police arrived, stopped the music and threatened to clear the premises if there was any further exhibition of 'western decadence'. Their savage attitude astonished me and I feared they might start clubbing people with their batons at any minute. While the armed policemen stood threateningly around the edge of the dance floor, the brass band reverted to staid waltz music and most couples quietly returned to their tables. We finished our beer and left. We had seen enough.

After I returned to England, the Russian souvenir badge remained for just a few days in the desk of my London office. Only people who understood the Russian alphabet would have known what it was. When it disappeared I guessed that our Secret Service agents had scooped it up during their nocturnal sweeps of the premises. In those days any English businessman who spoke Russian was suspect in the eyes of our Secret Service. Based on the fallacy that, 'as the foreigners are our enemies, he that speaks with the tongue of the enemy must be a traitor', they would now make an entry about the badge in their dossier on me. Although unjustifiably suspicious of me, the 'bungling amateurs' of our Secret Services actually worked for years alongside British colleagues who were not exposed as dangerous Soviet spies until they began defecting.

I carefully avoided the attention of the secret services on both sides of the Iron Curtain and, although the communists never tried to recruit me, our side attempted to do so on a couple of occasions. After falsely alleging that I was supplying machines to China for use in the production of atomic bombs, they attempted to force me into an espionage role. Later, they claimed to have information from their 'reliable people abroad' that I was working undercover for the Polish communist government and insisted that I became a double agent. When I rejected their cajoling approaches, they became threatening and interfered with my business affairs. As there was no truth in their allegations, I assumed that they must have been based on faulty intelligence. Years later, false intelligence, coupled with stupidity and deceit, would lead Britain into the ghastly Gulf War. I knew that our Secret Services were capable of wreaking vengeance on me for refusing to work for them and I thought that the most likely danger to me behind the Iron Curtain might come from their vindictive 'dirty tricks' department. I eventually took the precaution of no longer travelling alone and I kept away from the windows when in high buildings. Some of the more adventurous members of my staff were keen to observe life on the other side of the Iron Curtain, but others were reluctant because they found conditions there so dreadfully boring. Surprisingly, none of them complained of feeling under any threat from the communist authorities.

I became uneasy in January 1969 when the British Board of Trade issued a pamphlet entitled *SECURITY ADVICE ABOUT VISITS TO*

COMMUNIST COUNTRIES. The contents of that pamphlet were enough to deter anyone who had not been there, but seasoned travellers scoffed at the Board of Trade's advice. It all boiled down to a long-winded warning that, if travellers broke local laws, the communists might blackmail them and force them into espionage. No doubt the communists also issued similar advice to their visitors to Britain, because both sides used exactly the same vile tactics of sexual entrapment to blackmail politicians, diplomats, senior businessmen and others. The British pamphlets warned that the communist intelligence services sought 'information about western industrial developments and technical progress'. I thought, so what? That sort of thing is a normal activity in the cut-throat world of international trade. Every company in the world strived to learn the technical and commercial secrets of its rivals.

The world's fiercest competitors during the Cold War were the communist and capitalist powers. The disturbing thing was that the other side succeeded in obtaining so many of our industrial and military secrets, but we obtained so few of theirs. The communists had a distinct advantage, of course, while our Secret Service was riddled with top-level spies, like Kim Philby, who did not have to be blackmailed into betraying our country; they did so willingly.

The British Board of Trade regularly issued pamphlets entitled EXPORT INTELLIGENCE. They were intended to provide business leads in overseas countries, but were actually of little value. The silly people who issued them should have known that behind the Iron Curtain the word 'intelligence' was synonymous with 'espionage', so a more sensible title would have been something like *EXPORT OPPORTUNITIES* instead of *EXPORT INTELLIGENCE*. I warned my staff against taking the pamphlets abroad. I also warned my travelling men against black-market currency dealing – a practice that was prevalent in all the communist countries. Experienced western business travellers were able to circumvent many of the communists' tedious regulations and restrictions with the connivance of wily local citizens who were experts at the national game of outwitting their authorities.

CHAPTER TWELVE

Throughout the Cold War, the political system in the Socialist Federal Republic of Yugoslavia was the envy of the downtrodden people in the Soviets' satellite states. In 1944 I had repeatedly dropped parachute containers of guns, ammunition and explosives to Marshal Tito's resistance forces all over German-occupied Yugoslavia. Due to the mountainous nature of the terrain, and constant harassment by the partisans, the Germans were unable to control the whole country effectively. They merely maintained troops in scattered areas and attempted to combat the elusive partisans, who engaged in widespread 'hit-and-run' sabotage. In addition to dropping supplies for the partisans, I bombed such targets as German troop concentrations and railway marshalling yards. Most Yugoslav targets were within easy reach of our bombers' bases in southern Italy. My squadron's bombing and supply-dropping operations were carried out in close cooperation with the communist partisans.

Marshal Tito, the communist partisan leader, was to become the post-war Yugoslav President after eliminating the political opposition and uniting the country as a socialist federation. He distanced himself from his former Russian comrades in the Kremlin and became amicably inclined towards the western nations. Because of my wartime activity over Yugoslavia, I retained a keen interest in the people of that country and decided to visit all the places where I had dropped bombs and partisan supplies. My opportunity came after I opened a branch office in Milan (another of my bombing targets). During one of my monthly visits to my Italian office, I learned of possible engineering developments in the neighbouring Yugoslav province of Croatia, so I started to visit Zagreb each month. I based myself at the Esplanade Hotel (the wartime Gestapo headquarters) and quickly became acquainted with the local engineering enterprises. I had no great difficulty with the Serbo-Croat language as many words were similar to Russian and many Yugoslavs spoke the languages of their bordering Italians and Austrians.

I discovered that some of the local factory directors were ex-partisans and, when I informed them of my wartime supply dropping flights, they instantly regarded me favourably. One day, I was taken to a large empty field and told, 'We want to build a multi-million dollar manufacturing plant here. Are you interested in tendering for the project?' Although communist Yugoslavia was more prosperous than the countries behind the Iron Curtain, I wondered how the Yugoslavs thought they might finance such a large project. I need not have worried. The keen German, Italian and Japanese banks were quickly on the scene and I hoped the sleepy British would soon follow suit. Fortunately, they eventually did so and, to cut a very long story short, after many months of wrangling with buyers, suppliers and bankers, I secured a contract for more than £1 million sterling.

This first Yugoslav venture led to many years of further profitable business and, as a wartime supporter of the partisans, I soon gained favour with the Yugoslav industrial and political elite. The Party Chairman, the Finance Minister, the future Prime Minister, and other influential people became my close friends. The son of President Tito was the director of an engineering enterprise called 'First of May' and he became one of my valued clients. Incidentally, Tito was the name adopted by the partisan leader to disguise his identity during the war. His family name was Broz, but he retained the popular name Tito for the rest of his life. It was common for prominent communist politicians to adopt pseudonyms. For example, Stalin, Molotov and Gomulka were not the real names of those men.

My rapid social advancement eventually brought me into personal contact with President Tito and his wife. During our first meeting, I was so intent on promoting my business that I forgot to mention my wartime support for his partisans. However, judging by his friendly attitude, I guess, that Tito had already been briefed about me. Shortly after my meeting with Tito, his ambassador in

London told me that I should receive a medal for my wartime support of the partisans. I really had no interest in medals and I mentioned my wartime exploits merely to curry favour with my Yugoslav clients. Foreign trade was my main post-war interest. One day, a letter from the Cultural Secretary at the Embassy informed me that, 'As you did not serve in the Yugoslav National Liberation Army, you do not qualify for a medal.' I thought that 'National Liberation Army' was a rather inflated title for a band of brave, but ill-equipped, guerrillas who would not have been very effective without the substantial help provided by the Royal Air Force.

When I was dropping parachute containers of guns, ammunition and explosives to the partisans from a height of 200 feet, I had very little idea of what was happening on the ground. Typically, the secrecy-obsessed British authorities told us nothing more than the locations of our bombing targets and drop zones. They never informed us about the results of our efforts, but occasionally vague rumours from unknown sources circulated on our squadrons. For instance, we heard that the son of our Prime Minister was serving with the Yugoslav partisans, but few of us believed that story. We assumed that neither the Prime Minister nor his chiefs of staff would be foolish enough to risk the capture of a member of Churchill's family whom the Germans could hold hostage. However, our assumption was wrong. My friend, Wing Commander Cecil Harper, was the wartime Senior Operations Officer of the Royal Air Force's Balkan Air Force and he knew all about Winston Churchill's son Randolph. After the war, he told me:

> Before we knew anything about Tito, Prime Minister Churchill arranged for an officer named Fitzroy Maclean to be sent into Yugoslavia to discover which of the two main partisan groups was killing the most Germans. Maclean reported that we should support Tito's lot, and so we started sending over planeloads of supplies. Eventually, Randolph Churchill joined Fitzroy Maclean. I think his regiment in the Middle East was glad to get rid of him. I did not know Maclean personally; he seemed to be more of a political officer but, if he was

responsible for recruiting Randolph Churchill, I do not think he had much experience of selecting men.

The RAF set up several secret landing grounds in Yugoslavia under the control of tour-expired aircrew officers and, when the weather permitted, supplies were flown in and personnel were flown out. Cecil Harper told me:

> When we flew Randolph Churchill in, the Germans immediately attacked. Squadron Leader Bell was in charge of the landing ground and, to avoid capture by the Germans, he and the others had to take to the woods. Bell reported to me that Churchill proved to be such a menace that he would have shot him, if he had not run out of ammunition. When the Germans left, Bell and his men finally got back to the landing ground and I sent in an aircraft to evacuate them. Churchill pushed everyone out of the way and got into the plane first.

Strangely, Maclean seemed to overlook his friend Randolph's boorish behaviour.

We, who flew frequently over Yugoslavia with our bombs for German targets and supplies for the partisans, knew little about the dramatic events on the ground. We did not even know that Tito's partisans were at war with a pro-German partisan group that the American OSS still supported for a while after we had started to support Tito's lot. All we knew was that we should carry our revolvers in case we were shot down, because shooting ourselves, we were told, was preferable to falling into the hands of a brutal anti-communist group called the *Ustaše*. Flying over wartime Yugoslavia was described as like swimming across a crocodile-infested river. During my post-war business visits to Yugoslavia, I sometimes looked at my clients and wondered which side they had supported during the war, but I knew that the most important thing was their commercial support in peacetime. All other considerations were now irrelevant.

Cecil Harper was a fine source of information about wartime Yugoslavia. He told me:

> At one time, Tito was surrounded by Germans on the side of a

valley, so I sent in a Lysander piloted by a flight lieutenant of 205 Group. I think he had a double-barrelled name, but I have forgotten it. He landed in the valley, picked up Tito and then landed with him on the island of Vis with only one gallon of fuel left.

Without the timely intervention of the Royal Air Force, Tito would not have lived to become the Yugoslav President and the future of the Balkans would have been anybody's guess.

As the partisans had no access to hospital facilities, Cecil Harper frequently sent planes to evacuate the wounded to Italy. He recalled:

I received a message that two thousand wounded partisans needed to be evacuated within two days, otherwise they would have to be shot, because the Germans were approaching. We managed to get them out. Due to the scarcity of clothes, their fellow partisans had stripped them naked and wrapped them in blankets for the flight to Italy.

The Royal Air Force sent unarmed C-47 Dakotas to fly low while the crews threw out sacks stuffed full of uniforms and boots for the partisans. Unfortunately, one load of uniforms was too small to fit full-grown adults and one consignment consisted of left boots only. Inevitably, sacks of boots falling in darkness with the velocity of bombs injured some people on the ground. Steel supply containers weighing about 500lbs were dropped by parachute and their descent was quite rapid. On a daylight supply-dropping flight, I had skimmed over a plateau and descended to a height of 200 feet in a valley. Another plane had already dropped its containers ahead of me and, as the drop zone came into view, I saw a couple of hundred people standing around an area the size of a football pitch. About a dozen men and women started running out towards the containers lying on the ground and, as my plane approached slowly and quietly with its wheels and flaps down, I was relieved to see the people stop, look up and scamper away out of danger just as I pressed the switch to release my load of containers. They had a lucky escape. I was not prepared to declare a 'dummy run' and risk collision with another plane by aborting the drop and going round again. I could well understand why people were so keen to reach the containers. Even the parachutes were a great prize to be cut up and used as clothing.

As an example of my popularity with my Yugoslav clients, the general director of one large state enterprise provided me with an ancient American car and a driver so that I could tour the country at weekends. Occasionally, when the driver arrived at my hotel and asked where I wanted to go, I gave him some money and told him to keep the car and take his family out for a trip. No doubt he regarded me as a most generous English gentleman, but the truth was that I sometimes needed to stay in the hotel and catch up with some essential paperwork. Socially, my Yugoslav clients were full of fun and I thoroughly enjoyed their company. No matter how difficult the day's business negotiations had been, we always spent the evenings eating and drinking in a convivial atmosphere. While travelling around to places that had been my bombing targets and drop zones, I picked up quite a lot of valuable business. Although I often mentioned my air support of the partisans I tended to gloss over my bombing role because of unintended, or what later became known as 'collateral', damage. Occasionally, I slipped up. During my first visit to Energoinvest, a large electrical engineering enterprise in Sarajevo, the directors entertained me to a very wet lunch and then took me for a trip by car into the surrounding hills. As I looked down at the magnificent panorama of the entire city, I remembered how I had seen it in 1944. I said to one of the directors, 'I am trying to spot the railway yards; they are quite near the military barracks.' He turned to me with a quizzical expression, 'I thought you said this was your first time here.' I quickly changed the subject. The railway marshalling yards had been my bombing target in November 1944.

In a Sarajevo hotel, a man approached me and jabbered in a strange language that sounded a bit like Spanish. I told him in English that I could not understand him, and he replied in broken English that he had spent many years learning Esperanto and he was disappointed to find that nobody else understood it. When I said that English was more useful, he went away muttering that

Esperanto, not English, should be the world's language. I never met anyone else who spoke Esperanto and I assume that the artificial language has died out.

Although I spoke three languages fluently, and was able to guess my way through several others, I was glad when the use of English started to became widespread throughout the world. I secretly felt that the world might be a better place if we all spoke the same language and followed either the same religion or none at all.

I frequently travelled to Belgrade where street names and public notices were in Cyrillic characters. Thanks to my knowledge of Russian, I could read Cyrillic without difficulty. Another Englishman accompanied me on one occasion and when I spoke to a local official in my version of Serbo-Croat, I could read my companion's thoughts – 'bloody know-all'. The average Englishman resents fellow countrymen who talk in foreign languages without explaining exactly what is going on. I understand that feeling of frustration and that is why I avoided foreign interpreters, who often seemed to censor or abbreviate what the other party said. I could usually manage to communicate directly with all my foreign clients and this was sometimes achieved by means of a vocabulary concocted from an assortment of several different languages.

Travelling around Yugoslavia, I remembered things that my friend Cecil Harper had mentioned. As Senior Operations Officer at Brindisi, he had pilots of the wartime Croatian Air Force under his command. They came over to the winning side in 1944 and flew Spitfires on which they altered the red discs of the RAF roundels into red stars. I was hoping to come across some of those renegade wartime pilots, but I never found any. Perhaps none had returned home from Italy to an uncertain future under communism, or perhaps they had quietly gone to ground somewhere in Yugoslavia, fearing repercussions from the new regime. Who knows?

Cecil Harper also commanded a squadron of Royal Air Force BLAVS (British Latin American Volunteers). Most of those pilots, of British ancestry, were from Argentina. I doubt if they or the Croatian pilots got any official British recognition of their contribution to victory. They seem to have joined the vast ranks of unknown and unappreciated volunteers as soon as the shooting stopped. The Poles and Czechoslovaks, with a combined total exceeding twenty-five squadrons, were the most numerous foreign members of the Royal Air Force and their betrayal by their British allies has been well documented. Some other foreigners, who deserve to be mentioned, are the volunteers from neutral Ireland who were so numerous that people joked that if all the 'southern' Irishmen went home, the British Eighth Army would close down. One of the pilots of my bomber squadron had a navigator from neutral Ireland who, during his basic training in England, used to put on his civilian clothes and go back to Dublin on leave. When our squadron's casualty rate escalated, I admired him for coming back to share the danger with us.

During one particularly long period of contract negotiations in Yugoslavia, I developed severe laryngitis and was barely able to speak. My clients suggested a visit to a specialized clinic on the Croatian coast. The doctors there advised me to take a three-week course of treatment, but I explained that I could only spare one day. The treatment consisted merely of inhaling steam from a kettle of boiling seawater. There did not seem to be much improvement in my condition at the end of the day's session, but I was given a prescription for what translated as herbal tea. On the following day, I took the prescription to a local pharmacy and exchanged it for a large bag of dried herbs. During a coffee break at my client's offices I arranged for the herbal tea to be boiled like ordinary tea and, when a large bowl of the steaming brew was placed before me, I drank it. When I had finished, the General Director informed me with a barely suppressed grin, 'That was actually a gargle.' I was annoyed with myself for making such a silly mistake and I took the remainder of the bag of lightweight herbs into the lavatory, tipped it into the pan and tried to flush it away. Instead of disappearing, the stuff fluffed up and filled the lavatory pan. I flushed the pan repeatedly, but to no avail. The pan was still full when I left. I imagined how the cleaners might think, *'There must be something seriously wrong with that man's guts.'*

As I travelled around Yugoslavia I saw that walls everywhere bore the neatly painted inscription *ZIVIO TITO* in honour of the president. The graffiti was tidily applied as though with the use of a stencil, so I guessed that it was the work of the government. Nevertheless, Tito was undoubtedly a popular leader and many people said that nobody else could keep such a Balkan Federation united and peaceful. A factory executive told me:

I am a Muslim and my wife is a Catholic. We met when we were university students. We have never had any problems over religion, but I think our situation would be impossible without Tito in control of the country.

I often wonder what happened to that couple after Tito's death when the Federation split up in a frenzy of ethnic cleansing. During my travels through the country, I had occasionally detected a slight undercurrent of animosity between people of the various regions, but I thought at first that it might be nothing worse than such things as the English north/south divide and talk of Scottish independence. The directors of a large and successful Croatian enterprise complained that they were obliged to subsidize a subsidiary factory in an undeveloped area of Macedonia. Their attitude seemed to indicate religious and racial intolerance rather than mere financial considerations. After Tito's demise, armed conflict appeared to be inevitable and the British government's reaction was to appoint a failed English politician to intervene. I had about forty years' experience of dealings with Yugoslavs, so, believing myself to be far more of an expert on Yugoslav affairs than he was, I offered him some advice, but I think he resented my interference. I told him that ethnic cleansing would need to run its course before peace returned to the Balkans. Sadly, I was proved right.

In happier times, my wife was with me when the Yugoslav Finance Minister invited us to accompany him on a visit to the Lipizzaner stud farm at Djakovo. As a horse breeder, I eagerly accepted the invitation. He would have used his official car but, as I was not keen on the Yugoslav style of driving, I preferred to use mine. We set off with the minister sitting beside me in the front while his wife and teenage daughter rode with my wife in the back. He could not speak much English, but he continually urged me, 'Step on the gas.' I knew there was a strict speed limit, so I replied, 'Okay, I will step on the gas, but you must pay the fine if we get caught.' He laughed, 'Step on the gas.' I guess he had learned the expression from an American gangster movie. Very soon, we were hauled over by a motorcycle cop who approached the open window on what he thought was the driver's side and he instantly recognized my important passenger. With a broad smile, he said 'Good day, Comrade Minister' as he handed over a speeding ticket. After the Finance Minister paid up, we continued our journey at a more moderate speed and there were no further urgings to step on the gas. The minister's daughter said, 'Father appears so often on the television that everybody recognises him. We see him more often on the television than we do at home.' I am sure that he had never been fined for speeding before. No cop would dare to stop his distinctive chauffeur-driven official vehicle and now he had learned what driving was like for the rest of us.

Upon arrival at Djakovo we transferred into a carriage drawn by two smart Lipizzaner horses and attended by liveried coachmen for the final part of the journey to the stud farm. The director of the stud received us with a speech of welcome and conducted us around the establishment. Everything was spotlessly clean. One of the grooms in smart livery tacked up a horse for me to ride and, in the evening, a lavish banquet was arranged in our honour. Although I knew that the Finance Minister was an important and popular person, I wondered why my wife and I were also being treated as such important guests. When I signed the visitors' book on the second day of our visit, I learned that the Queen and the Duke of Edinburgh had been invited to call at the stud farm after an official visit to Belgrade and our visit was a full-dress rehearsal for that important occasion. We departed from Djakovo with a car-boot full of bottles of *Slivovice* (plum brandy) and complete legs of *Prsut* (hams that had been wood-smoked up the chimney).

As often as possible I tried to trace the locations of the wartime secret landing grounds used by the Royal Air Force during the German occupation of Yugoslavia. According to Wing Commander

Cecil Harper, the Russians had a landing strip near one of ours in Montenegro and one evening a British airman accompanied a Russian on a drunken visit to a nearby village. Their respective authorities detained both men and the next day the officer in charge of the British contingent visited his Russian counterpart and suggested that both men should receive identical punishment. The Russian officer agreed. He added, 'We shot our man at six o' clock this morning.' Discipline among the partisans was equally harsh. While men and women shared the same primitive accommodation, sexual intercourse was banned and execution was invariably the punishment when sexual relationships were discovered.

In 1941 Wing Commander Cecil Harper had been an acting pilot officer (the lowest commissioned rank) and by 1944 he had operational control of several squadrons of C-47 Dakotas, B-24 Liberators and Halifaxes, all of which were engaged on the dropping of supplies and agents into enemy-occupied territory all over the Balkans and northern Italy. One day he received a phone call from the RAF's Balkan Air Force headquarters informing him that they were sending him two fighter squadrons. He told me:

> I had controlled bombers in the UK and the special duty squadrons in Italy, but I had absolutely no experience of controlling fighters; however they said I would just have to cope, so I sent the fighters to attack concentrations of enemy troops and transport. I told them where our secret landing grounds were situated and said they should make for them if shot down.

The fighter pilots wore heavy army boots in case they were shot down in the mountains and they carried a Sten gun for their protection on the ground. In addition, they had a knife to stab the rubber dinghy if it accidentally inflated in the cockpit. They were far better informed and equipped than we were on our bomber squadron. Although we bombed and dropped supplies all over the Balkans, we did not even know that the landing grounds existed. We had no army boots. My only pair of shoes had holes in the soles and, in wet weather, most of us were obliged to wear our flying boots on the ground as well as in the air. We had no Sten guns for personal defence, but we each had a revolver and six bullets for the sole purpose of shooting ourselves. Nobody told us anything except the locations of our targets and drop zones. We never knew exactly where the front line was. One dark night, on the way back from an attack on a target in France, we attempted to cross the Italian coast at Leghorn (Livorno) and were met with such an intense anti-aircraft barrage we had to flee out to sea and make another attempt further south. Our fools had not told us that the Americans had just taken Leghorn. Neither did they tell us about the French underground resistance forces in the south of France. We assumed, at the time, that all the Vichy French were obedient lackeys of the Germans. We did not know that my friend Cecil Harper actually had a squadron of French fighter pilots under his control. We did learn, however, that he controlled a squadron of Italian pilots who had recently changed over to the winning side. They flew their own Italian fighter planes when they escorted us for a daylight raid on Sarajevo in November 1944. The Italian escorts were indistinguishable from our enemies who were flying identical planes. We viewed that situation as a minor irritation compared with the other more deadly 'cock ups' that we regularly encountered. Some of my worst frustrations were caused by hopelessly wrong weather reports. We loathed our Met Officer and treated him like a fool when he asked us at debriefing what the weather had been like. It had rarely corresponded with his misleading forecasts of fine weather.

In the late summer of 1944 a contingent of the Soviet Russian Air Force arrived at Bari in southern Italy and Cecil Harper took operational command. He now had Russian-built versions of C-47 Dakotas plus Yak fighter planes under his control. He told me:

The Russians were commanded by a Ukrainian general. He moved into Bari's Imperial Hotel and I got on well with him. As an interpreter, I had an assistant – a Canadian flight lieutenant of Ukrainian extraction whose parents had settled in Canada. I did not have to use the Canadian as an interpreter very often, because several of the senior Russian officers spoke a little English. I was quite familiar with Russian customs because I had been married for a while to a Russian actress from Georgia and we had a number of prominent Russian friends while I was at Cambridge University. In those days, I knew the Russian prince who was the first husband of the wealthy Barbara Hutton. She prospered greatly by marrying again after he was killed in a car crash. I also knew the Russian prince who was implicated in the murder of the Czarina's confidant, Rasputin. I got on well with the Russians at Bari socially, but I found them difficult to control operationally. Their flying discipline was strict, however, and, regardless of any difficulties encountered, they dared not return to base without successfully completing their supply-dropping operations. Incidentally, they only had their terribly thick Russian uniforms to wear in the heat of the Italian summer and I heard that they were paid in American dollars at an even higher rate than American airmen were. When it was time for me to leave Bari and return to Brindisi, the Russian officers gave a dinner in my honour with numerous toasts in vodka and *slivovice*. I was sitting next to the Russian commander and I asked him what he would do after the war. He said that, as a Ukrainian, he was not a Stalinist and he had no idea what he would do. Then he continued chatting and mentioned that the Russians had already lost over eighteen million men, so they might have to retain their German prisoners to use for breeding purposes and he thought the German government might allow men to have several wives, because they were also short of men. I wondered if the matter had any relevance to his post-war plans.

I doubted that the Russian commander would last long after returning to Russia. My guess is that the men in the Kremlin would not welcome home a senior Ukrainian officer who might have been under the influence of 'western decadence' during his time in Italy. I knew that I would never discover what happened to him, but I looked forward to meeting other Soviet airmen in due course.

CHAPTER THIRTEEN

During an early business trip to Poland, I unexpectedly encountered more Russians than I had bargained for. On a Friday afternoon I finished my business meetings in Wroclaw. My next appointments were scheduled for Monday morning, so I was free until then to explore the countryside. I looked at my map and noticed that Hitler's pre-war autobahn passed just south of Wroclaw and came to a stop a few miles further on. At the time of the autobahn's pre-war construction, Wroclaw had been a German town named Breslau – the capital of Silesia. After Churchill and Roosevelt had allowed Stalin to retain the illegally-invaded eastern half of Poland, they compensated the Poles by shifting the Polish border westward into German territory as far as the line of the Odra/Nysa Rivers. The Poles then moved into the German territory, unceremoniously kicked out the German inhabitants and changed the names of the towns.

It was a pleasantly warm Sunday morning and, having nothing better to do, I decided to drive to the end of the autobahn and see what it looked like. I was glad to be on my own after a hectic week of haggling with officials of the state purchasing authority. The road was completely clear of traffic and weeds growing through cracks in the concrete showed that it was out of use. I stamped on the accelerator pedal to blow the carbon out of the engine and enjoyed an exhilarating burst of speed. Suddenly, the autobahn terminated in a huge mound of sand. There was nowhere else to go, so I turned around and drove back past Wroclaw until I saw a town on my right. The signs showed the town's name was Legnica. As I drove through the main street, I looked forward to stopping for a beer and then, to my surprise, I saw that the centre of the town was crowded with hundreds of dejected looking Russian soldiers. There seemed to be no civilians around and I guessed that Legnica must be an important garrison town. While some soldiers wandered aimlessly around the streets, others stood chatting in groups. They reminded me of our own poorly-paid wartime soldiers overseas – spent up, fed up and homesick. I parked the car in front of a café, sat at a table outside and ordered a beer. I was the only customer. I watched the occasional lorry passing by with its Russian inscription CA, denoting that it belonged to the Soviet Army. Then a couple of Russian versions of jeeps slowly crept along the street while armed military police looked out at the soldiers with the same sort of hostile facial expressions that I had seen on military policemen all over the world. My shiny new luxury car with its GB sticker looked totally out of place in the street and I expected to be challenged by the military police at any moment. I watched as a couple of inquisitive soldiers bent down to peer through the car's windows. As I sipped my beer I ran over in my mind how, if challenged, I might explain to the Russians that I did not know that Legnica was a garrison town – I arrived there by chance while out joy-riding. I thought they would not believe that and if I spoke in Russian they might suspect me of spying, so it might be better to play the foolish lost Englishman and merely ask for directions to Wroclaw. To my surprise, nobody actually approached me, so I tried to look nonchalant when I strolled over to the car, casually got in and drove away through deserted side streets. I had discovered by pure chance where the Russian occupation army was situated in Poland's newly-acquired former German territory, but I was actually far more interested in the Red Army's past activity in the same area during the dark days of 1945.

By February 1945, the last significant obstacle facing the troops of the Red Army was the river Oder and after crossing that, they would be only about sixty miles from Berlin. Stalin's advance seemed unstoppable and his uncooperative attitude to his western allies made them fear that the Red Army might eventually end up in the port of Calais on the French coast. By 14 February the Red Army had taken Breslau (now Wroclaw). It was then only about eighty miles from the poorly-defended German city of Dresden, where hundreds of thousands of homeless refugees were sheltering. By that time, the combined force of the British and American strategic bomber offensive had reached the peak of its awesome destructive power. In the pretence (to the public) of attacking military and industrial targets, our bombers were carrying out the western Allies' policy of massive area bombing to destroy German towns and sap the morale of the civilian population. As the Red Army advanced, the British and American bombers wiped out the city of Dresden, killing and maiming untold thousands of its unfortunate civilian inhabitants.

Perhaps the bombing of Dresden at such a late stage of the war was intended to demonstrate our terrifying air strength to Stalin, rather than to assist the Red Army's advance. After seeing what we had done to Dresden (and could do to Moscow), perhaps Stalin would not want to challenge us so aggressively over the post-war carve-up of Europe. Whatever may have been the reason for the massive slaughter of Dresden's citizens during the closing stages of the war, the bombing unfortunately reflected discredit unfairly on my fellow airmen.

After finally concluding my business negotiations in Wroclaw, I decided to drive through Dresden on my way back to England. It was late afternoon when I entered the city centre and parked my car in what seemed like the biggest car park in the world. There were no other cars in sight and, in the fading afternoon sunlight, my GB sticker openly proclaimed my identity as a citizen of the country jointly responsible for Dresden's destruction. I hoped that neither the car nor I would suffer retribution from any surviving local residents whom I might encounter. I walked along streets that were lined with the skeletons of ancient, prestigious buildings. Dresden was a city of oppressive gloom and the most profound silence. No bird sang, no dog barked, no music played. The city was devoid of motor traffic and, as I watched a few shabby people wandering slowly across an empty square, the ghostly scene was like a horror movie. I became aware that the city had a faintly unpleasant smell and, in consequence, I was taking unusually shallow breaths. This first visit to Dresden had thoroughly sickened me and, within half an hour, I was glad to resume my journey, safely cocooned in my British car. The winding road from Dresden brought me onto the crumbling autobahn that led from the miserable conditions of Russian-occupied East Germany into the areas occupied by the western Allies. There was a stark contrast between conditions in East and West Germany. While towns in the east remained in a state of utter dilapidation, the West Germans worked by day and night, clearing rubble and restoring buildings. The West Germans showed no sign of animosity towards the British and American armies of occupation, obviously welcoming the troops as a ready source of cigarettes, chewing gum, coffee and other valuable commodities. The British 'no fraternising' rule was soon disregarded by the troops. 'I can get a bunk-up with a young Frau for a packet of cigarettes and a bar of soap,' a British soldier told me with a grin. 'It's better here than back home.' The black market flourished like nowhere else, and the British and American troops had the time of their lives.

During the early 1950s I frequently drove non-stop through West Germany because overnight accommodation was almost non-existent in the devastated towns. I once attempted unsuccessfully to find a place to stay in Mainz where, for miles, the ground-floor shells of ruined houses were full of brick rubble shovelled up out of the dusty streets. Pathetic wartime slogans, painted on the walls, proclaimed in German, 'Every sacrifice is for victory' and 'They break our walls but not our hearts'. The word 'they' applied to my young aircrew friends and me. We resented being branded as *Terrorflieger* (flying terrorists) for obeying orders based on Allied bombing policy, when refusal would have resulted in court martial proceedings and imprisonment. I encountered no personal animosity from the German people and I found myself sympathizing with them, just as I did with all other victims of the ghastly air war.

My squadron in Italy bombed enemy aerodromes, oil refineries, railway marshalling yards, harbours, canal installations and enemy troop concentrations. I was totally unaware of the Allied policy of massive area bombing carried out from British bases until my wife and I visited Cologne shortly after the war. We stood near the cathedral and looked askance at the surrounding devastation and at the masses of '*Schwerbeschaedigte*' (severely disabled people) with their black and yellow armbands. We had never seen anything like that before. I was shocked and I whispered to my wife, 'What on earth have we done?' It was even more of a shock when I discovered that our bombers had done the same thing all over Germany and, although I had not participated in area bombing, I felt ashamed of my own wartime role. I assured my young wife, who had met me while I was still in uniform, 'I never did anything like this. I only carried out precision bombing of specific targets. I never bombed through cloud or on ETA and I never bombed the wrong place.' Despite my protestations of non-complicity, I still felt guilty. I knew that, just like my friends who destroyed Cologne and Dresden, and the German airmen who attacked lovely towns like Bath, we had all obediently complied with our superiors' commands. We were like inanimate puppets with callous old men jerking the strings. Our manipulators shamefully turned their backs on us later when the true horror of our actions was revealed. After the attacks on Dresden, Winston Churchill referred to Bomber Command's raids as 'acts of terror and wanton destruction'. Arthur Harris, the head of Bomber Command, vigorously protested that Churchill's remarks were insulting. Regardless of the questionable ethics and effectiveness of area bombing, Harris had acted in accordance with the bombing policy dictated by his political masters and, like his bomber crews, he was cruelly discredited for obeying orders. Royal Air Force bombers were in continuous action from the beginning to the end of the war. Enemy action caused the deaths of over 55,000 RAF bomber crewmen. (The American casualty rate was even higher.) Additionally, untold thousands became casualties as the result of crashes during training flights. Controversially, no bomber campaign medals were issued and Winston Churchill, who paid glowing tribute to the efforts of munitions workers in his victory speech, disregarded entirely the efforts and sacrifices of the bomber crews.

After taking early retirement from the Royal Mint, where war medals were manufactured, an acquaintance came to work for me. He asked if I knew why the Mint produced campaign stars, instead of round medals.

I said, 'Perhaps because stars look more attractive.' He told me,

'The reason why the government decided on stars was because stars require less metal than discs.'[1]

A fellow veteran bitterly remarked, 'That's typical of the penny-pinching people who even swindle our wounded men out of war pensions.' Incidentally, medals were not issued automatically. The veterans had to submit written applications; otherwise, they did not get any medals. Predictably, some men did not bother to apply and, equally predictably, the medals received by applicants, three or four years after the war, did not always correspond with the applicants' entitlements. Cock-ups galore! Many of my Czechoslovak and Polish friends received neither medals nor even ribbons from official sources and I supplied scores of bits of ribbon to them after the eventual collapse of their communist regimes. In Prague, one of the RAF's Czech veterans gave me a copy of a letter sent to him in 1945 by our War Office at Droitwich Spa. The contents of the letter were as follows.

Sir,

I am directed to forward the ribbons of the 1939-45 Star and the Africa Star awarded to you for service with the British Forces in North Africa.

It is understood that by the acceptance of a British Campaign Star or Medal you will not be entitled to a similar award from your own government, or any other allied government; that is to say a Campaign Star or Medal instituted for the period and service for which a British Star or Medal has been granted. The continued wearing of the ribbons will be invalidated by the acceptance of any other award as above defined. The Stars will not be made at present, but when ready they will be sent to your Government Headquarters for disposal. You should, therefore, inform your Government of any change of address and quote the above reference number in all correspondence about the Stars.

I am, Sir,
Your obedient Servant,
(Signature – L. Jolliffe.) Director of Personnel Services.

Although, when he received the letter, the recipient was still serving as a sergeant in the Royal Air Force and the letter bore his RAF number, he was addressed as 'Private, Czechoslovak Army'. After demobilization, he returned to his home town in Czechoslovakia where he faced communist persecution as punishment for his service in our air force.

British medals were not available for general distribution until about three years after the war had ended and, by that time, the Soviet Union had taken control of Czechoslovakia and Poland with the callous agreement of the British and American governments. Men who returned home in their thousands after serving voluntarily with the British armed forces were branded as enemies of the state and flung into communist prisons. Shamefully, our timid government made no sign of protest to the villainous Stalin, who was still being placated long after the Cold War broke out.

During the summer of 1944 I carried out several night-bombing raids on the Bucharest/Ploesti oil refineries. Our casualties on seven-hour trips to the Rumanian oilfields were high and whenever the pink tape on the large map at briefing led to Ploesti a silent feeling of dread pervaded the atmosphere. The Ploesti oil refineries were designated the number one priority target in Europe and enemy opposition there was intense. We bombed the refineries at night and our American colleagues, flying from the same airstrip at Amendola, bombed them in daylight. Our squadron's unofficial pecking order was linked to our record of attacks on such dangerous targets as Ploesti, rather than on our air force ranks. As Ploesti veterans, we felt vastly superior to those who were not, but we secretly recognized that our survival was largely a matter of pure chance.

Long after the war, I was chatting to a young American A-10 pilot at an international air show. I mentioned that my old wartime squadron flew American B-24 Liberators. When I told him that we bombed Ploesti, he yelled to his colleagues, 'Hey guys, this gentleman bombed Ploesti.' The other young pilots rushed over to shake my hand and, as they listened to my account of our attacks, I recaptured the half-forgotten feeling of achievement shared by all my squadron's Ploesti crews during those bygone days. The name of Ploesti plays a significant role in the wartime history of the American air force but, sadly, not in ours. The former British military attaché in Bucharest told me, 'When I noticed a lot of Royal Air Force graves in the Bucharest cemetery, I wondered what those airmen had been doing in Rumania.' How shameful! Our hazardous attacks on oil targets undoubtedly contributed more to victory than attacks on any other targets, but our military attaché had never even heard about us and the slaughter of our long-dead colleagues.

In investigating the possibility of doing export business in communist-controlled Rumania, I hoped that business trips would give me the opportunity to visit more of my wartime targets. In 1944 my crew had made a dangerous lone flight to drop supplies to a group of sailors who were sent to blow up the Iron Gates of the Danube. The secrecy-obsessed British authorities did not allow us to know whether or not the saboteurs were successful or even if they got the supplies. Understandably, the Rumanian communist authorities would not allow me to travel to the sensitive Iron Gates area that bordered Yugoslavia, but I did succeed eventually in visiting all the places where I had dropped bombs. On the first of many business visits to Rumania, I booked into Bucharest's impressive Athenee Palace hotel. Business negotiations with officials of the State Trading Organization were at first unproductive, but the city of Bucharest was delightful, despite being under the heel of a brutal communist dictator. In the afternoons, when I had no more business engagements, I strolled over to the nearby Lido Hotel. While I sat at a table beside the pool, drinking Soviet champagne and observing dozens of scantily-clad young Rumanian women, the madness of the Cold War with its threat of mutually assured annihilation seemed like a faraway concept. I was fortunate in being able to enjoy visits to magnificent cities like Bucharest, Prague and Budapest in the days before the blight of mass tourism, obtrusive public advertising in the streets, fast food restaurants and burger bars marred their old-world charm. The fact that the villains in the Kremlin ruled over most of central and Eastern Europe did not deter me, and while most of my timid western competitors stayed away, I rapidly expanded my export business.

While visiting the scenes of my wartime bombing, I met five Rumanian pilots who had flown German Ju88s and Bf109s in defence of the Ploesti refineries and we spent many hours reminiscing about our respective flying experiences. The Rumanians were keen to hear all about the wartime Liberator bomber and I learned about the characteristics of their Ju88 and its tendency to ground loop. As we chatted in the manner typical of ex-aviators all over the world, it was difficult to realize that we had been intent on killing each other a few years ago.

I was able to guess a bit of the Rumanian language and Bulgarian was not much of a problem, but I found that Hungarian was one of the world's most perplexing languages. However, as most government officials could speak German, that was the language used for business negotiations. All Hungarian waiters and taxi drivers also understood German, so over the years I only picked up half a dozen Hungarian words. As a linguist, I felt that I really ought to learn at least how to pronounce the names of my wartime targets correctly so, in conversation with an elderly gentleman in Budapest, I wrote down and asked him how to pronounce the names of places like *Szombatheley, Hajduboszormeny, Miskolc* and *Szekesfehervar*. As I tried to say the words properly, he enquired, 'How do you know so many places in our country?' I said, 'I learned those names during the war.' I did not tell him that the unpronounceable names belonged to places that I had bombed when Hungary was allied with Germany. He asked excitedly, 'Were you a spy?'

He was clearly disappointed when I said I had not been a spy. I have no doubt that, like most other people, he was far more interested in tales of wartime espionage than in the exploits of bomber crews. Writers of popular fiction misleadingly portray the sordid business of espionage as adventurous and romantic, whereas during the Cold War it was, in many cases, bungling and ineffective.

It was impossible to travel extensively behind the Iron Curtain without encountering the shadowy world of espionage, assassination and subversive propaganda. My accountant, Dave, had served in the Intelligence Corps of the British Army during the war. Towards the end of hostilities, he was engaged for a while on some kind of mysterious task in Bucharest where he married a local girl who was related to a prominent anti-communist politician. After the war, Dave's wife made British propaganda broadcasts to Rumania. Both she and Dave were supporters of an anti-communist dissident group in London. One evening, Dave's wife found him dead in his armchair when she returned from work. He had not been ill and I suspected that he might have been assassinated. The communists were intolerant of émigrés who broadcast information to their people behind the Iron Curtain and I knew that an apparently accidental bump by a person on a stairway or in a lift could disguise a fatal injection and, as a result, the victim died of an apparent heart attack. Understandably, I tried to avoid involvement with dissident groups on both sides of the Iron Curtain. Assassination methods were many and varied. Georgi Markov was a Bulgarian émigré who paid with his life for broadcasting BBC propaganda to his fellow countrymen. As he stood on the pavement in the vicinity of London Bridge, an unknown assassin pierced his leg with the tip of an umbrella and inserted a fatal dose of ricin poison. He was not the only person in Britain to suffer an attack with deadly ricin. In time, assassination methods would include the use of radiation poisoning of foreign dissidents in the very heart of London.

I heard numerous allegations of wartime political assassinations during my travels behind the Iron Curtain and one of the stories, spread by some Poles, was that Winston Churchill had instigated the murder of their political and military leader, General Sikorski.

On Sunday 4 July 1943, Sikorski and members of his staff, including his British liaison officer, Colonel Cazalet, boarded a B-24 Liberator in Gibraltar. The plane took off at 11.00pm with the United Kingdom as its intended destination but it crashed into the sea as soon as it was airborne. Every time I heard allegations that Sikorski's death was not an accident, I informed the Poles that it was not unusual for Liberators to crash immediately after take-off. I knew what I was talking about because identical crashes had occurred on my Liberator squadron in 1944. Furthermore, I heard that there were a few Liberators in the sea at the end of the runway at Brindisi. I discussed the rumours about Sikorski's death with Count Edward Raczynski, the wartime Polish Ambassador in London. He told me that he noticed Winston Churchill weeping during Sikorski's funeral service in London. Hardly the behaviour of an assassin!

In every country behind the Iron Curtain, the state controlled the newspapers, radio and television. The censors opened and examined postal correspondence and microphones were installed in public restaurants, hotel rooms and even in foreign embassies. Telephones were bugged and duplicating equipment was unobtainable by ordinary members of the population. Nevertheless, a surprising amount of information circulated secretly behind the Iron Curtain. When the Soviet Union announced that they had sent an officer named Gagarin, allegedly the world's first astronaut, into space, my Czech clients informed me that the report was false. They told me:

> Gagarin was not the first astronaut. A Russian named Ilyushin was previously sent into space and lost for a while in a capsule that went out of control. He screamed in panic when he realized that the controllers were having difficulty in retrieving him.

Apparently, he expected to suffer the same fate as the little dog named Laika that the Russians had sent into space with no possibility of its survival. The Czechs said:

> Although Ilyushin did eventually return to earth, he and his space flight were disregarded and the more politically acceptable Gagarin was later feted as the world's first spaceman.

I was surprised that the Czechs were able to obtain information that the Russians kept secret from their own people and the rest of the world. There is no doubt that the Russians' achievements in space acted as a spur to the Americans in their race to put the first men on the moon, but I wonder if that American achievement did anything to promote world peace.

As the Cold War continued unabated, it seemed to me that the men in the Kremlin were set to reign over their Soviet empire for hundreds of years. The Russians opened a trade legation in the London district of Highgate and, during Harold Wilson's term as British prime minister, the prospects of trade with the Soviet Union improved considerably. When a British trade association encouraged its members to participate in an international engineering exhibition in Moscow, I picked up a business visa from the Russian Embassy, booked a room at Moscow's prestigious Hotel Ukraina and bought a first-class ticket on Russian Aeroflot. At London's Heathrow airport I boarded the Aeroflot plane and asked the steward to direct me to the first-class seats. He replied, 'Everything on Aeroflot is first-class, so you can sit anywhere you like.' Consequently, I sat with people who may have paid much less for their tickets than I had. I remembered the communist slogan, 'from each according to his means'.

As a Russian speaker I was looking forward to the trip. My vague preconceptions of Russia were falsely based on my studies of great literary works by authors who lived in bygone days of elegance. I should have known better and I was in for a shock. Upon arrival at Moscow airport, the passengers were shuttled from one bus to another. I mentioned that I had booked a room at the Hotel Ukraina and I was told that my booking had been transferred to the Ostankino Hotel, which appeared to be a former army barracks. I alighted from the bus at the same time as an elderly Russian émigré who owned a furniture factory in England. He had come on the trip with the sole intention of visiting his elderly sister in Leningrad, but he learned upon arrival at the airport that his visa restricted him to Moscow, so he would be unable to leave the city. Moreover, Russians from other districts were not allowed to enter Moscow, so he would not be able to see his sister. He had left Russia before the Bolshevist revolution and this was his first taste of communism. We arrived at the Ostankino at the same time and, despite our protests, we were shoved into the same room. My elderly companion complained that the doorman did not hold open the door or help him carry his luggage into the hotel. The worst was yet to come. At nearly midnight, we struggled along a bare concrete corridor to our room while vowing to complain again in the morning.

In the room we found much more to complain about. We were on the ground floor and there were no curtains at the windows. Carousing people were passing by and staring into the room, so we switched off the light before undressing. The washbasin was full of dirty water and the plughole was blocked. The wastepaper basket was full of rubbish and the floor was filthy. I went down the corridor to a communal washroom and toilet where conditions were equally disgusting. Early the next morning, I stormed into the reception office and bellowed in Russian at all those present. I said that I had stayed in hotels all over the world and even in the poorest third world countries I had not experienced such deplorable conditions. I shouted, 'You people are a disgrace to the Soviet Union.' They told me that there was no alternative accommodation available and I said that, although I did not object so much to sharing a room, I would not tolerate such filthy conditions. I added, 'If this is a typical example of Soviet Russia, I can only say it stinks.'

I knew that insulting the Soviet Union was a serious criminal offence and I wondered if I had gone too far, but I was past caring. I told them, 'I will tell Khrushchev about this when I see him.' I was bluffing, as I did not really expect to meet him. However, my empty threat seemed to make an impression on them and they told me that there was a spare bed in a room occupied by an Englishman in another (barrack) block and they assured me that it was not dirty. I moved into the other room after dark. There was nobody there so I got into the spare bed, put out the light and pretended to be asleep when the Englishman returned. Squinting through almost closed eyes, I saw him stare down at me for a few seconds and then turn away with a troubled look on his face. I would deal with him in the morning.

My new roommate was ready for me when I awoke. 'Now look here,' he said in an aggrieved tone, 'I am a senior British civil servant and this room is paid for by the government. We are not allowed to share. You should not be here. I cannot share the room with you.'

My response was, 'That is your problem, old chum, I am staying.'

I guessed that he was a junior civil servant. I did not think that a senior British official would be staying in the crummy Ostankino. I did not see him again, so I now had a clean room to myself.

Breakfast at the Ostankino was a revelation. The dining-room staff were obviously tough Russian soldiers dressed as waiters. The choice of breakfast food was omelettes, poached eggs, fried eggs or scrambled eggs, overcooked and served in individual aluminium dishes. I ordered scrambled eggs, but got two fried eggs instead. When I pointed out to the waiter that I ordered scrambled eggs, he picked up my fork in his ample fist and vigorously churned up the two fried eggs in the dish. 'There,' he declared triumphantly, 'Scrambled eggs.' Thoroughly scrambled they certainly were. I could not argue about that.

There were about a dozen British company directors present at the international exhibition and we were invited to attend the opening ceremony. We stood outside in front of a crowd of Russians, unaware of what would happen next. A load of officials arrived in a cavalcade of huge black limousines and suddenly a dozen security guards in civilian clothes appeared and charged at us like American football players. Without uttering a word, they slammed their shoulders into us, forcing us back half a dozen paces. As we were being flung back there was much indignant muttering from the Englishmen and cries of protest from the people behind us whose feet we inadvertently trampled upon. A few minutes later, Khrushchev appeared with a beaming smile and performed the opening ceremony. I doubt if the Soviet leader gained any English friends that day. A few days later, one of the English directors had his camera confiscated when he photographed wooden huts that were being cleared away to make room for the erection of huge concrete apartment blocks. The police accused him of gathering propaganda material with which to discredit the Soviet Union. He thought he was recording progress. Another member of the English delegation was deported from Moscow for telling some Russians that they were fools for putting up with the communist regime. Criticism of the regime was such a serious offence I would not have been surprised if he had been sent off to join dissidents in a Siberian gulag.

Free speech was unknown in the Soviet empire. Several Russians dared to ask me, 'Can people say what they like at Speakers' Corner in Hyde Park?' Others asked, 'Are English people allowed to criticize your government and demonstrate in the streets?' I had the distinct impression that Russians, who had known nothing but the oppressive communist system since birth, received my answers with a certain amount of scepticism.

I found that officials at the Ministry of Foreign Trade viewed me with suspicion when I spoke Russian. During commercial and technical discussions, they tried to negotiate using their own interpreters and attempted to stop me speaking directly to their engineers in Russian. My reaction was to bombard the interpreters with rapid English colloquialisms and slang until they were totally flummoxed. Not being able to translate English technical terms relating to advanced production processes, the hapless interpreters soon pleaded, 'Please explain that in Russian.' I then stopped speaking English, by-passed the interpreters and talked directly to the engineers in their own language. Without the hindrance of the interpreters, our negotiations speeded up considerably. The engineers were happy with the situation, but the commercial officials snarled, 'Why do you speak Russian?' I asked sarcastically, 'Would you prefer me to speak Norwegian?' Fortunately, they did not say yes, because my knowledge of Norwegian comprised no more than about ten words. I enjoyed the joke, but they looked annoyed.

The high point of the trip to Russia was an invitation for about ten of us to join Khrushchev at a reception in the Kremlin. After an impressive tour of magnificent buildings to view priceless artefacts, including gifts to Czar Nikolai from Queen Victoria, we were seated at tables where each guest had a bottle of red wine, white wine, cognac and vodka. The food was excellent. I have never seen such a lavish spread. Conditions in the Kremlin were vastly different from those endured by the unfortunate people outside. Khrushchev was not a man of impressive appearance, but he was certainly charismatic. His presence filled the vast banqueting hall and he obviously enjoyed taking centre stage. Most prominent Russians were great drinkers and maybe the effects of vodka accounted for his ebullient manner. He spoke to us in Russian with the use of an interpreter. I have never heard anyone else use an interpreter so skilfully. His timing was perfect – pausing in exactly the right place to allow the interpreter to catch up, before delivering his punch line. He was like a first-class comedian and his performance was impressive. There was an undercurrent of deadly seriousness as he chided us over our government's allegedly hostile attitude to the 'peace loving' Soviet Union. It was clear that we were in the presence of a clever, ruthless and powerful man. I doubted that our own politicians were capable of dealing with him. I waited the whole time for him to say something in Russian to his henchmen that was not intended for our ears, but that did not happen. He was far too crafty.

At the end of the international exhibition, the members of our delegation were invited to visit an engineering factory where a few British-made machines were in use. I looked forward to talking to the factory workers. I stopped when I saw a large British machine and asked the operator, 'What do you think of this machine?' I was particularly interested because it was manufactured by one of my suppliers. To my surprise, he said, 'We had to take the table off.' The large reciprocating table weighed fifty tons and the machine was barely three months old. Before I could say anything else, the official interpreter accompanying our group rushed over to me and shouted above the noise of the machines, 'No time for talking. Come away.' I tried to explain that I needed more information. There should be no need to lift a fifty-ton table off a machine that was still under guarantee. The manufacturers should be notified of the circumstances. 'Come away. No time for talking,' the interpreter insisted. I reluctantly rejoined the group and each time I spoke to any of the workers the interpreter hustled me away again, insisting that there was no time for talking. I was puzzled. We were in a quite ordinary engineering factory. It was not an ordnance factory or any other kind of secret establishment, so I wondered why I was not allowed to speak to the workers. A few days later, the reason dawned on me. As a new development, the sliding surfaces under the fifty-ton reciprocating table were lined with a patented low friction material. The Russians had never seen that material before and they apparently wanted to investigate it. If they had asked me I would have sent them a sample. It was freely available for export. By dismantling the table they had infringed the terms of the manufacturer's guarantee. No wonder they did not want me to talk to the workers!

For the next factory visit we had a different interpreter. As our group assembled, he asked, 'Does anyone speak Russian?' Thinking he wanted some help, I stepped forward. He looked through his list and told me, 'There are too many people, so you cannot go with us.' The other members of the group boarded a half-empty bus and departed without me.

I felt sorry for the British technicians who spent a week setting up their exhibition stands and then manned them for twelve hours every day for three weeks. No evening meals were available at the Ostankino, so the men had to travel into the centre of Moscow after work in search of food. Several times I accompanied them and acted as interpreter. By the time I had finished translating the menu they had forgotten what was supposed to be available and I had to start all over again. I had difficulty in remembering what each man wanted, so I wrote it down on a paper serviette. A waiter saw my scribble and asked me to let him have it. He assured me that he could understand my Russian handwriting, so I did the same thing on subsequent occasions. Eventually, I saved time and effort by announcing to the men, 'You will all get beetroot soup, crab salad, steak, beer, coffee and vodka. I cannot keep going through the entire menu for you when half of the items are not available.'

Nobody complained, but the service was painfully slow and it was always about midnight by the time we finished eating. The next problem involved getting taxis back to the Ostankino Hotel. Late at night, hordes of vodka-soaked drunks staggered around the streets and every taxi queue was like a rugby scrum. When taxis pulled up at the head of the rank, the drivers shouted out words like Kazanski Vaksal and people wanting to go in the direction of that railway station fought their way to the front of the queue and scrambled aboard. In the mad rush it was difficult for us to maintain our places in the queue. I shouted that it was our turn next as drunken louts pushed us out of their way. When I protested and they heard me speaking to my group in English they snarled, 'As guests in our country, you should show us some respect.'

One night I struggled through the usual hostile crowd and got into a taxi. Then a drunken brute grabbed my arm and hauled me out into the gutter. I scrambled up off my knees and was on the point of hitting him when two others stepped forward and I had to back off. There was never any police presence on such occasions after dark. Towards the end of our time in Moscow, when the technicians were packing up their exhibits, I invited the English group to join me for a midday meal and I booked a private room in a state-controlled restaurant. We ordered soup and the only meat dish on the menu. While waiting for the meals to arrive, we stoked up on vodka and beer. By the time the food eventually appeared we were all cheerful and relaxed as we swapped tales of our experiences abroad, and told jokes. There was nothing wrong with the soup and bread, but the meat was so hard and tough that we could not even cut it, so we knew we would certainly not be able to eat it. Suggestions were made that it might be dog, goat or bear. One man took photographs as another posed with a knife in one hand over the meat and a bottle as a mallet in the other hand. In an atmosphere of great hilarity, men changed places and more photographs were taken.

At the end of the photo session a waiter appeared and I told him that, as the meat was inedible, we would like more soup, bread and beer instead. He replied, 'You will get nothing more here. We know you have been taking propaganda photographs to discredit us.' Despite my protestations, he was adamant. '*Nichevo*, No soup, no bread, no beer! You have insulted us.'

As we had been alone in a private room with the doors shut, it was obvious that we had been under secret surveillance the whole time. None of the Englishmen understood Russian, so I explained the situation to them and told the waiter to bring the bill. It was about an hour before he re-appeared and, in the meantime, we found that we were securely locked in. While we waited, we talked in hushed voices and wondered if the police were on their way to arrest us. When the waiter eventually re-appeared, we resentfully paid the bill and then he unlocked the doors.

As we walked away from the restaurant, vowing never to return, I heard my companions' comments, 'I don't understand why the Russians are so bloody touchy.' 'They obviously don't understand the British sense of humour.' 'I have had a bellyful of this place. I hope I never have to come back here, it's like a vast prison camp.' 'I feel sorry for the people who have to live here.' 'Bloody Russia – it's definitely not my cup of tea.' The remarks prompted rueful laughter as the men recovered from the day's chastening experience.

I knew that it would be unwise of me to try to meet any war veterans or talk about military matters, but I was keen to meet people and learn more about life in Russia. Most Russians seemed wary and suspicious of me, but I had better luck talking to university students in the street. Their attitude to me was uninhibited and friendly. They were curious about social conditions in the West and about pop music and trends in modern dress, but politics and the Cold War were never mentioned. None of them had met a Russian-speaking Englishman before and, as I spoke Russian without the use of modern slang words, I asked them if they found my Russian stilted. They laughed and pointed to a swarthy companion. 'You speak much better Russian than he does,' they told me, 'He only learned Russian in order to study at the university.' They were referring to a fellow student from one of the many countries of the Soviet Union where Russian was not the first language of the population. Unlike London, Moscow's streets and parks were completely free of litter and the Metro was spotlessly clean. I learned from the students that if anyone dropped a cigarette end in public someone would pick it up, hand it back to him and tell him to use a litter bin. I asked the students if religion was banned in Russia and I learned about the teaching of a subject called Anti-Christ. The students told me that only old people attended church services. People who wanted to sing in a church choir had to join a union, but many old people could not afford the union dues. Churches had to have fire insurance and if the congregation could not afford to pay for it, the church had to close. When priests died, those from neighbouring areas had to share the deceased priests' duties and when the extra work became too arduous, more churches had to close. When they told me that the state appointed the bishops, I said, 'I am not sure, but I think it is the same in England.'

I found that the students were far keener to learn about conditions in the 'Free World' than they were to discuss details of conditions in Russia. In the unforeseen future those Russian students would be able to shake off some of their government's oppressive political controls while, regrettably, the British people's freedoms would suffer a significant decline.

On my last day in Moscow, a man sidled up to me in the street and whispered, 'How many shoes, shirts and suits have you brought with you to Russia?' I asked him why he wanted to know and he recited a list of prices in roubles that he would pay for those items. Black market dealing was a serious criminal offence and I guessed he might be either a well-dressed black market dealer, possibly in cohorts with the police, or a policeman trying to entrap me. When I spoke to him in Russian he swiftly scampered away.

When our British delegation arrived in Moscow, we had been obliged to declare and convert all our money into travellers' cheques that were only valid in Russia. We were assured that any unused cheques could be converted back into hard currency at the airport before we departed. However, we found on departure that the money change kiosk was shut and we were left with worthless cheques and another grievance. One of my most sickening memories of Moscow was the sight of Ted Hill, President of the British Boilermakers Union, locked in a mutual embrace with Khrushchev.

Bureaucracy, dictatorial officials and continual frustrations had blighted my trip to Moscow and, as I boarded the plane to London, I vowed never to return. Later, I discovered that the rooms in Moscow's Ukraina Hotel were fitted with devices for keeping guests under surveillance and, as my booking was not honoured, I assume that at that time the Russians did not consider me important enough to warrant bugging. Some time after my visit, Greville Wynne, a fellow British businessman, was overheard in his room at the Ukraina as he talked to Colonel Oleg Penkowski of the KGB.

Penkowski was providing secret information to the British through Wynne. During a subsequent trip behind the Iron Curtain, Wynne was snatched off the street and bundled into a car. Some of my business acquaintances were with him at the time and, thinking that criminals had kidnapped him, they reported the incident to the British Embassy. They told me later that Wynne had often hinted that he was a British secret agent, but they thought he must surely have been joking. He was not joking and the unfortunate fellow appeared on the television in tears at his trial in Russia. The following year the Russians arrested Penkowski, and he was reported to have been tortured and then executed.

Soon after my return to London, I received a letter from Moscow inviting me to return there to finalize contract formalities. I replied that I would only return to Moscow if a visa also permitted me to visit a stud farm at a place named Ternopol. When, as expected, I was told that my visa would restrict me to the city of Moscow, I declined the invitation and told the Russians to negotiate through their trade legation in the London district of Highgate. My refusal to return to Moscow resulted in all future contracts being negotiated through the mail. The fact that the Russian trade legation in Highgate was not involved, and that the people there showed scant interest in trade, strengthened my belief that it was nothing more than a front for an espionage centre.

My interest in a visit to the stud at Ternopol came about in the following circumstances. For a time, the Russians had sent riding horses to the Lincolnshire port of Boston with shiploads of timber. According to the local British veterinary surgeon, some horses arrived with broken legs and they were transported back to Russia in that condition. All the uninjured horses were auctioned off at prices of around £60 each. One particularly striking young stallion made eight times the average price. Although he was a beautiful horse, he proved to be so dangerously wild as to be unsuitable for the average rider. I bought him and began the long task of re-schooling him. On the first day, a visiting friend helped me to lead him into the stable where we spent two hours trying to get a bridle on him. After mounting him outside, I found that he preferred to rush madly backwards instead of going quietly forward. He spooked at everything and would not tread in a puddle or walk over a pole on the ground. However, after two years of persistent retraining, I succeeded in making him into a perfectly well-behaved horse, and I could take him hunting and show-jumping. On his first day out with the Old Surrey and Burstow Foxhounds he jumped thirty formidable obstacles and then, as he stood quietly among one hundred other horses waiting for the hounds to draw, a fellow hunt subscriber remarked, 'What a well-mannered horse!'

According to the official documentation issued by the Russian Ministry of Agriculture, the horse was bred at Ternopolska stud farm and his breed was Ukrainian Saddle Horse. His documents included a certificate bearing the surprising statement 'has passed initial training'. During my overseas travels, I had seen some rough treatment of horses and I now wanted an opportunity to investigate what I suspected to be harsh training methods at the Ternopol stud farm but, when I found that I was not permitted to visit Ternopol, I openly declared that I would never visit the Soviet Union again.

Although I never made contact with Russian military personnel in the Soviet Union, I had no difficulty in meeting high-ranking officers when we stayed in the same hotels as guests of the Polish and Hungarian Governments. The Russians, mainly colonels and generals, were amongst the most friendly and good humoured people I had ever met, and I welcomed the opportunity to use my ability to socialize with them in their own language. In Warsaw I received a gold medal from Russian General Antanov, a veteran of the battle for Berlin and in Budapest a similar medal from another general whose name escapes me. I can well understand why our British Secret Service was suspicious of me. I undoubtedly had more good contacts behind the Iron Curtain than they had and they were certainly aware of that. I repeatedly refused their forceful 'invitation' to become a double agent. It was not an attractive proposition. They told me, 'There will be no remuneration and if you are caught, we shall have to deny all knowledge of you.' I could not believe that they could recruit suitable people under such conditions. Their final words to me were, 'Woe betide you if our paths should ever cross again.' Fortunately, I am not easily intimidated and I never became either a double agent or any other kind of secret agent.

In view of Russia's turbulent history, I could understand the Soviet government's distrust of foreigners, but their secrecy seemed excessive when even a stud farm was 'off limits'. To some extent, however, the Soviet Union's suspicion of the Western powers was justified. Before my trip to Moscow, an American pilot named Gary Powers was shot down while flying a U-2 spy plane over Russia at 70,000 feet. Other NATO planes regularly probed the airspace of Warsaw Pact countries and Royal Air Force planes were sent to investigate Russian long-range aircraft on their way to Cuba. Flying in close proximity to the Russian planes, the British pilots sometimes held up copies of saucy Playboy magazines that were unobtainable in Russia. An English pilot told me that he sometimes gave the Russians a demonstration of his Lightning aircraft's astonishing ability to perform vertical climbs. All this activity may have seemed like a game to the pilots concerned, but accidents can happen. I know of incidents during the Second World War when pilots inadvertently opened fire or collided when performing mock attacks on each other. I had no doubt that such an accident involving a Russian plane would have serious repercussions and I could see no sense in needless provocation.

Khrushchev had valid reasons for suspicion of the British since he and his colleague Bulganin sailed to Britain on their cruiser *Ordzhonikidze* for a 'goodwill' visit in 1956. Khrushchev complained to the British government when our Secret Service sent a frogman named Buster Crabbe to investigate the underside of the Russian vessel in Portsmouth Harbour. Crabbe's attempt failed and a decapitated body, assumed to be his, was later washed up on the coast. Exactly how Crabbe lost his life is a mystery, but a Secret Service blunder was assumed to be responsible for the tragedy. While the British Board of Trade was urging people like me to promote trade with the Eastern Bloc, it seemed that officials in some other government departments were intent on antagonizing the men in the Kremlin.

When Harold Wilson became our prime minister he appeared to be a great admirer of the Soviet Union and it was difficult to distinguish the socialists from the communists in his administration. He was a great supporter of trade with Russia and I remember his sycophantic praise of the Russians during a luncheon of the Russo-British Chamber of Commerce. The United States had appointed itself as the world's most obsessive anti-communist power and had taken on the task of attempting to stamp out the spread of communism wherever it appeared. I assumed that, in the event of war, the Americans would need Britain as an aircraft base and I wondered how they might view the prospect of a communist-led British administration. Disturbing rumours began to circulate in London's pubs and clubs, and I feared that the Americans might eventually intervene to prevent a communist coup. One of a number of London's hotbeds of rumour and gossip was a fashionable Belgravia establishment within a short distance of Buckingham Palace. There the names of senior military men and a distinguished member of the Royal Family were bandied about in relation to a possible overthrow of the prime minister. Rumours emanating from the same source indicated that the people of MI5 were behind a plot to oust Wilson and, after he suddenly resigned, he accused them of complicity in his downfall. As the upper echelons of our Secret Service were riddled with traitors, I guessed that they would not have acted against Wilson unless coerced by the CIA (American Central Intelligence Agency).

In the dirty world of international espionage during the Cold War everything was possible, including blackmail and murder. When the British secret services made determined but abortive attempts to recruit me as a 'double agent' they assumed that I was already spying for their Cold War enemies. They apparently based their assumption on faulty intelligence as the communist security services had never approached me and I had always steered clear of them. Many years later, faulty intelligence would mislead the British people into believing that the Iraqi president had access to weapons of mass destruction that could imminently be launched against us. After a great deal of bloodshed during the ensuing conflict, it became clear that no such weapons existed.

My work took me to all the continents of the world in pursuit of international trade. My life was a continual round of foreign automobile plants, aircraft factories, steel mills, shipyards and various other engineering works. I stayed in the finest hotels and ate in the best restaurants all over the 'Free World', but my insatiable curiosity repeatedly drew me back to countries behind the Iron Curtain, where I had strong wartime connections. I never tired of hearing accounts by local people of what was happening on the ground while our planes flew overhead with their loads of deadly bombs for the enemy or supplies for the resistance forces. Some of my best sources of information were the veterans of the Polish underground resistance forces. Knowing that I had flown to Warsaw during the 1944 Uprising, they treated me like a hero. One of them said, 'We admire you for helping us because it (the Uprising) was not your fight, but yet you volunteered to bring us guns and ammunition during that terrible time.' A myth had developed among the Poles that the Royal Air Force crews had volunteered for the hazardous flights to Warsaw. The truth was that, although all our British aircrews enlisted voluntarily, it was not customary for us to volunteer for any particular flights. In fact, 'off his head, or flak-happy' was our usual description of anyone on my squadron who volunteered for anything. Volunteering was regarded as tempting fate, so we just did as we were told, and we certainly did not volunteer for the hazardous Warsaw flights.

I have no doubt that the intrepid men of our Polish squadron at Brindisi may have volunteered to fly to Warsaw, because they knew that the future of their capital city was at stake. We had heard about some of their daring exploits and we regarded them as crazy. One night a Polish crew flew around waiting for a signal from the people on the ground. There was no sign of life on the designated drop zone, and the normal procedure in such circumstances was for the aircraft to return to base with the supplies that had been intended for the underground resistance soldiers. However, as it was Christmastime, the crew decided to drop the supplies into a nearby village as a present to the inhabitants. During interrogation back at base, the crew were reprimanded for not obeying orders, but then a radio message from Poland reported that the villagers had handed over the supplies to men of the resistance forces who were hiding from the Germans in the locality.

We and the Polish crews dropped not only supplies, but also secret agents into enemy-occupied territory. All the crews on the special duties squadrons had men called despatchers, whose duties included shoving out kitbags full of unbreakable supplies for partisans through the gaping hatches in the floors of Halifax aircraft and supervising supply dropping through the bomb doors of Liberators. The despatchers also supervised the dropping of secret agents into enemy territory. Static lines attached to Liberators and Halifaxes automatically opened the agents' parachutes. On one occasion, the static line did not detach from the parachutist and he dangled helplessly below the plane. The Polish despatcher was unable to haul the poor man back into the plane and he could not leave him suspended outside, so he grabbed the aircraft's fire axe and chopped through the static line. Back at base, he was asked to explain his action and he said:

> I did what I had done previously when I had the same trouble with parachute containers of supplies. I severed the static line. There was no alternative and he was going to die whatever I did.

A Polish airman, who related this incident to me, said, 'After debriefing, the despatcher was taken away and we never saw him again.' I assumed that the parachutist was one of the important Polish politicians who were dropped into Poland. I also wondered if the despatcher became an innocent scapegoat when equipment failure was the true cause of the parachutist's death.

Every time I visited Poland during the Cold War, veterans of the Armia Krajowa bombarded me with information about the structure of their wartime underground organization and its resistance to the German occupation. I learned that every time the resistance forces killed a German soldier, the Germans took reprisals against innocent Polish men and women who were rounded up indiscriminately and gunned down in the streets. Consequently, the fear of reprisals caused the underground forces to become unpopular among some sections of the civilian population. After each massacre of civilians, the Germans put up posters in the streets listing the names of the people they had shot. Other posters listed the names of hostages in detention who would be shot in reprisal for any further attacks on German troops. The lists of hostages often contained the names of complete families. One afternoon my Polish friends took me to a place they called the tramway. It was a building where the Germans had detained people indefinitely on chairs arranged in rows exactly as though they were on a tram. The victims were not allowed to move from their seats and their tormenters repeatedly prodded them with batons in the region of the kidneys until urine streamed down their legs.

Despite German reprisals, and scant support from the British government, the activity of the Armia Krajowa continued. The British Foreign Secretary still insisted that the Poles be restricted to only enough air-dropped weapons for minor sabotage purposes; otherwise they might use them against Stalin's troops. Although Britain had entered the war in support of the Poles, they received no help whatsoever from Britain apart from the pitifully inadequate 600 tons of supplies dropped by planes of the Royal Air Force. (The French resistance received about 10,000 tons.)

When the Polish émigré government repeatedly complained that advancing Red Army troops were disarming and persecuting members of the Armia Krajowa, the British government reacted with fierce anti-Polish hostility, fuelled by fear that the Polish attitude to Russia was detrimental to British political negotiations with Stalin. At the same time, many thousands of the Polish émigré government's brave soldiers were dying alongside men of the British forces in places like Arnhem and Cassino.

I was reminded that the Polish underground forces included hundreds of women combatants when, in Warsaw, I was introduced to a rather frail lady who had been a member of the group responsible for the assassination of SS General Franz Kutschera in February 1944. Announcements emanating from Kutschera had been regularly broadcast over loudspeakers in Warsaw's streets. Although the announcements were intended to intimidate the population and turn people against the Armia Krajowa's actions, the sabotage and killing of the German occupation forces continued and, eventually, it was the turn of SS General Kutschera, 'the hangman of Warsaw', to be assassinated by an intrepid group of Armia Krajowa soldiers. I was proud to meet a lady who had played an active part in the assassination of one of Hitler's cruellest villains. My lasting impression of her is of a refined person whose modest manner belied her heroic past.

Publisher's note:

1 Stars were the traditional form of campaign medal, dating back to the issue of the Kabul to Kandahar Star in the 1880s. The economy made in 1945 was to issue Second World War stars in brass rather than the more expensive bronze and not to engrave the recipients' details on the reverse. Before this the only unnamed award was the Ashanti Star of 1896, of which only about 2,000 were issued.

CHAPTER FOURTEEN

While I was negotiating some important contracts in Prague during early 1968, Dubcek, the new Party Chairman, was attempting to introduce 'Socialism with a human face' to the Czechoslovak people. I noticed a general air of cautious optimism among the population as the 'Prague Spring' continued, but I felt pessimistic and I warned my Czech friends that their masters in the Kremlin would certainly not allow them more freedom than they allowed their own people. By April, most Czechs seemed untroubled by the Kremlin's disapproval of the changes being introduced by Dubcek and Prague's hitherto gloomy atmosphere gave way to an almost festive mood of optimism but, remembering the brutal crushing of the Hungarians in 1956, I felt that Dubcek's quiet revolution would not last long.

After a sales tour of Hungarian and Czechoslovak factories in April 1968, I was due to travel from Prague to Katowice in Poland with two of my men and a fully-equipped mobile demonstration workshop. I already had a Polish visa but the Polish Embassy in London had refused to issue visas to my companions. 'Don't worry. That's no problem,' I told them. 'I know a man in the Polish Consulate in Prague who has all the necessary rubber stamps for granting visas. Bring your passports and we'll go and see him.' The Consul explained that he was not allowed to issue any visas until further orders and that all the Polish borders were closed. I protested that I had received an urgent telex message requesting us to visit a Polish steelworks and there would be ructions if we failed to appear. I dropped the names of important people in the Ministry of Trade in Warsaw to impress him and he asked me to show him the telex message. I said, 'I will bring it tomorrow morning.' No such message existed, so I went back to the Alcron Hotel and sent a telex to the director of the Polish steelworks requesting an appropriately worded reply. A telexed reply was received from the steelworks within an hour and I returned to the Consul and urged him to issue the visas. He reluctantly complied, but remarked, 'I cannot see how these visas will help you when the borders are closed to all traffic.'

We set off at daybreak the next day and I deliberately chose the minor border crossing point at Nahod – hoping it would be unmanned. There was no immediate sign of life when our vehicles arrived at the border but, within a few minutes, bleary-eyed Czech and Polish border guards scrambled out of their shared customs house and announced that the frontier, marked by a single flimsy red-and-white-striped wooden pole, was closed. I flashed my gold-embossed British passport with its multitude of visas and, putting on a typically British-style show of false indignation, I insisted on proceeding unhindered. I pointed out that, as British citizens, we should not be inconvenienced when going about our legitimate business. 'Your president will hear of this,' I blustered, 'Where is the telephone? I want to speak to the minister in Warsaw.' A young woman in uniform said, 'It is not our fault. Don't blame us; we are Czechs, not Poles.' The Poles said, 'Anyway, the documents for your vehicles are not in order, so we would not let you proceed even if the border was not closed.' We knew that they were lying and, after a couple of hours of argument, we produced a selection of ball pens, playing cards and chocolate bars for the Czech officials.

The Poles gradually became less obstructive, so we included them and eventually they raised the barrier and let us through into Poland. Within a couple of hundred yards of the border we came across masses of tanks, manned by what appeared to be Mongolian troops. They did not interfere with us. They were obviously poised to invade peaceful Czechoslovakia. I had seen no sign of defensive preparations on the Czech side of the border, so I assumed that the invasion would be unopposed and the Czechs would probably not face the same fate as the Hungarians.

Surprisingly, the expected invasion was postponed and my business trips behind the Iron Curtain continued normally. In Poland, people seemed unaware that their own troops were on standby for participation in the invasion of their neighbours and, although still living in a police state, the Poles seemed to be enjoying a slight easing of the restrictions placed on them by their communist masters. People could now apply for exit visas for short visits to western countries, but the state bank allowed them to take abroad no more than the equivalent of two pounds in hard currency and somebody, such as a relation in the West, was required to provide a written invitation guaranteeing to cover all costs abroad. To deter people from defecting permanently to the West, married couples were not both allowed to travel abroad together or with their children.

From April until August 1968, the Soviet troops remained in the region of Czechoslovakia's borders while the Kremlin exerted severe political pressure on Dubcek and his ministers.

In August I was in Austria, driving my car towards the Czech border, when the Kremlin's troops eventually invaded with tanks and planes. Two of my men accompanied me with our mobile workshop. My assistant, Tom, a multi-lingual ex-wartime airman, was undeterred by news of the invasion and it was clear to me that both of my companions regarded the trip as an interesting and adventurous departure from our usual visits behind the Iron Curtain. There was no thought of turning back, so we proceeded in the wartime air force spirit of 'press on regardless'. Meanwhile, the Czechs had opened their borders and fleeing refugees streamed out into Hungary and Austria. At the border, I discovered that hordes of fleeing Czechs had illegally exchanged their money for a pittance in Austrian currency. In the West, the Czech money was hardly worth more than its value as scrap paper, so I decided to buy some and smuggle it back over the border. The Austrian bank officials were delighted to accept a few hundred British pounds from me in exchange for an enormous amount of Czech money. As I left the cash desk the Austrian bank clerk whispered conspiratorially, 'You should not let the Czech customs officials know that you have this money.' I grinned at him. I was gambling that the Russians would not introduce occupation currency and make my hoard of Czech money worthless.

I stuffed all the Czech notes into a large innocent-looking wooden toolbox and proceeded over the border to the Czech customs house.

Our side of the road was completely devoid of traffic, so the customs formalities did not take long. A female official climbed into the mobile workshop and kicked the box containing the money. It was not locked. I expected her to ask, 'What is in there?' but instead she turned to me with a grin and said, 'I suppose that is full of Czech money.' I pretended not to be listening as I casually handed over our passports and the vehicles' documents. I then unhurriedly entered the customs house, and handed out packs of American cigarettes and bottles of coke to each of the officials. I did not mention the Russian invasion and neither did they. There were no Russian troops at the border, but I expected to encounter some at our next stop in the town of Brno. Surprisingly there were no Russians in Brno either, but I found that news of the invasion had caused great consternation among my local clients. My Czech friend Jan told me:

> My wife panicked when she heard on the radio that the Russians had landed at Prague airport. She immediately went out and converted all our money into goods. She even bought herself a fur coat and now we have no money at all. I don't even have the price of a beer.

I had known Jan for about ten years. He was normally a jovial individual and, as a director of a local engineering factory, he was an important client. I had never seen him looking so down in the mouth, but I had the remedy. I said, 'Come and see what I have for you in the vehicle.'

As I shoved a bundle of Czech money into his hands, I said, 'I have repatriated this lot. It was exported illegally. Bring your wife and her sister to the Grand Hotel about six o' clock. We are going to celebrate over dinner with a few bottles of Soviet champagne.'

I actually had no need to contravene the currency laws because my company met all our expenses, but taking a risk at the border gave me the same irresistible adrenalin rush as that to which I had become addicted during my flying days. The RAF's psychoanalysts thought that aircrews were too stupid to appreciate the dangers of operational flying, but they were wrong. The truth was that many of us could not resist the challenge of confronting dangerous situations and we remained that way (a little crazy perhaps) long after our flying days were over. Business people travelling behind the Iron Curtain were subject to a multitude of regulations and restrictions, and our attempts to outwit the communist authorities added spice to routine trips.

Travel behind the Iron Curtain, with its element of danger, was full of surprises. One day my Austrian friend Karl and I were engaged in business discussions with the general director of a large Czechoslovak enterprise who mentioned rather wistfully that his parents had often travelled by tram for an evening's entertainment in Vienna before the war. He asked me, 'Have you ever been to the famous Folies Bergère in Paris?'

I told him that I had a branch office in Paris and I frequently took clients to the nightspots.

He said, 'We have never had the opportunity to visit those places and we have nothing like them in our country. The authorities do not allow such things as striptease, but we sometimes arrange quite interesting private parties for a few friends. We can arrange something in your hotel apartment this evening, if you like.'

I consulted Karl. He knew that director better than I did and he assured me, 'It will be alright because the General Director will be with us and he is one of the top communists in this region, so there will definitely be no trouble from the police. By the way, we will need some Tuzek coupons for the girls.'

After dining with three of our clients in the hotel restaurant, we sent a supply of drinks and snacks to our apartment and the private party got under way. Half a dozen attractive young women arrived and the General Director took on the role of master of ceremonies. The radio played quietly in the background, drinks flowed freely and, in the dim lighting that was a characteristic of all hotels behind the Iron Curtain, the apartment took on a typical smoky night-club atmosphere.

I asked one of the directors, 'Where did you find these girls?'

He told me with a grin, 'We know all of them. They are medical students from the university. These are some of the prettiest ones and there are plenty more where they came from.'

While chatting to one of the girls, I learned that she was due to qualify as a surgeon in a few weeks' time. I also learned that, under the communist system, there was no shortage of doctors and they were of no higher social status than skilled workers such as plumbers.

About an hour after the girls arrived the 'master of ceremonies' announced, 'There is a prize for the girl with the biggest tits.' The girls promptly stripped off their tops and lined up with their bare chests puffed out. After much deliberation we selected the winner of that competition and, a few drinks later, a further announcement was greeted with great hilarity. 'Now there is another prize, but this time it is for the girl with the smallest tits.'

As the evening progressed, more competitions took place with the enthusiastic participation of the girls until the party finally broke up at about two in the morning. Karl and I pooled our Tuzek coupons and shared them out among the girls. The Tuzek coupons, obtainable only by westerners in exchange for hard currency, could be used to purchase duty-free goods at the Tuzek shops. Czechoslovak citizens were forbidden to own hard currency, but with gifts of Tuzek coupons they could buy goods that were unavailable in ordinary shops. Alternatively, the coupons could be sold very profitably on the black market, so they were ideal gifts. As the General Director prepared to leave, he shook hands and said to me, 'I am sure this evening was not comparable with what they have in Paris, but it is the best we can do here.'

I replied, 'Actually, this evening was a lot more fun than anything in Paris. Let's do it again sometime.'

After loud laughter and mutual back-slapping, the general director said as he departed, 'I will see you in my office at around ten o' clock.'

Before turning in, I opened the windows of the apartment for a few minutes to let out the strong smell of tobacco smoke, *Becherovka*, *Slivovica*, wine and Soviet champagne.

Karl grinned at me, 'That certainly was quite some party.'

I joked, 'It was just another one of the hazards of foreign trade.'

We both knew that our good friend the General Director would do everything possible to expedite the large contract for British machines that we were negotiating. We also knew that we were all flouting a multitude of the communist government's regulations but, as I often remarked to Karl, 'It is far better than being bored to death.' We took many risks and faced countless difficulties behind the Iron Curtain. Boredom was never a factor.

In August 1968 I mentioned that I intended driving to pick up a British colleague at the airport and three of my burly Czech clients insisted on accompanying me as bodyguards. They warned me, 'Russian troops, camped in the region of the airport, are robbing the occupants of cars. They only take Czech money, not foreign currency or travellers cheques. They want Czech money to buy vodka. You will not have any trouble if we are in the car with you.'

My Czech friends were right. We were not stopped. On the way to the airport, I saw young Russian conscript soldiers standing disconsolately around their primitive mobile kitchen equipment and I felt sorry for them. They probably had no idea why they were stuck there, isolated, miserable, poorly paid and hundreds of miles from home. Young soldiers of every nationality know that feeling of helplessness, despair and homesickness. I would have liked to stop and talk to the Russian troops, but I knew that my Czech friends would object, so I drove on. I was unable to share the Czechs' hatred of those ordinary Russian soldiers. I said, 'The bastards in the Kremlin are to blame for the political situation, not these poor sods here – they have to do what they are told, whether they like it or not and I am sure they don't want to be here.'

I sensed that the Czechs were disillusioned and disappointed by the leaders of the Soviet Union. For years, there had been no visible Russian presence in Czechoslovakia. By and large, the population had been fairly compliant and most people had not shared the Polish people's fierce anti-Soviet attitude. After all, the West had betrayed the Czechs and the Russians had liberated them from the Nazis. Now, in 1968, the Czechs appeared to be friendless and isolated.

When the Russian troops arrived in Prague with tanks that crashed through barricades of trams and private cars, they encountered indignant men and women who surrounded the tanks, and berated the bewildered soldiers who seemed to think they had been sent as liberators to restore order. Some Czechs climbed up on to the tanks and shoved bunches of flowers into the muzzles of the guns. Other Czechs argued angrily in Russian with the tank crews who seemed baffled by the general population's hostile attitude. The Czechs turned their signposts round to confuse the invaders and the words 'Ivan go home' were daubed in Russian on walls everywhere. Dramatic reports appeared in the western press of Czechs being shot by Russian troops. I did not witness any shootings, but I have no doubt that the Russian soldiers would have obediently fired on the population, if ordered to do so.

Red Army soldiers had driven the Germans out of Prague in 1945 and a statue of the heroic Russian General Konev still stood unblemished in the city. After the 1968 invasion, I saw that a Russian tank that formed part of a memorial to Russian soldiers killed during the wartime liberation of Prague had been disrespectfully daubed all over with pink paint. While sympathizing with the Czechs, I was sad to see evidence of such an inappropriate act of vandalism. Like many other war veterans, I cannot condone insults to the memory of any nation's war dead, no matter what may be the nature of later international disputes. The Czech leader Dubcek failed in his attempt to develop a liberal form of socialism and Soviet troops remained in permanent occupation although, apart from an occasional military vehicle, I saw nothing of them in the towns. When travelling between Czechoslovakia and Poland, I perceived a distinct cooling of political relations between the two neighbouring countries and I became aware of the Czech people's resentment of the Polish government's military support of the Russian invasion.

I once had occasion to apply for a visa at the Czechoslovak consulate in Warsaw. As I started filling in my details on the visa application form, the Czech consul advised me, 'If you are a journalist, don't put that down on the form. These days, it is better to describe yourself as an engineer.' I replied, 'As a matter of fact, I am an engineer.' He grinned at me, 'Oh yes, I bet you are.'

Remarkably, my business activity continued with scarcely any interruption throughout the invasion of Czechoslovakia and its aftermath. The same situation had existed in Poland during the 'bread riots' over the government's intention to increase food prices.

It seemed that neither the Kremlin's Cold War disputes with the West nor clashes within its vassal states could disrupt the vital process of international trade.

CHAPTER FIFTEEN

My business visits to the communist dictatorship of Rumania enabled me to see the Ploesti oil refineries and other places that I had bombed, but at first the visits proved commercially unproductive, so I turned my attention to Bulgaria, one of the Soviet satellite states that was completely new to me. Although Bulgaria had supported Germany during the war, I had not dropped any bombs there and, on my first visit to the capital city of Sofia, I was 'cold calling' without any commercial contacts whatsoever. I booked into the Balkan Hotel that was reputed to be the best one in Sofia. When the porter showed me to my room and unlocked the door, I noticed a snag. The room was completely without furniture, so we returned to the reception desk and collected another key.

As the lift was out of order, we had to climb up the stairs to the top floor where, after traipsing along a dusty corridor, I was shown into a small room with en suite bathroom. The rusty bathtub looked as though it had not been used lately, so I wandered around until I found a woman working in another room. I led her to my room, showed her the rusty bath and asked her to clean it. The next snag was that no water came out of the taps, so I returned to the reception desk and explained the situation to the porter. He told me to get my soap and towel, and follow him. We arrived at the room of another guest and the porter knocked on the door. When the door opened, the porter said nothing to the room's occupant, but he told me, 'You can share with him.' He then turned on his heel and walked away. I found that it was customary in communist countries for hotel guests to be treated as though they were in the army. Sometimes, total strangers were bunged into rooms together, regardless of their nationality. In the Balkan Hotel's restaurant I got into conversation with a group of Polish men who were on a coach tour with a young female courier. They told me:

The organization of this trip is chaotic. Instead of double rooms, there are nine of us in one room and we are sharing with the courier. We go to the room, get into bed first, and try to pretend that we are asleep when she gets undressed. Last night, we all had a lot to drink, but we tried to keep quiet when she came in to the room. Then, when somebody did a loud fart, several men started laughing and she got annoyed. Today, she is sulking and not talking to us.

My first meeting with officials of the Bulgarian State Purchasing Authorities was held in the open air on the concrete steps outside the building. There was some rather lame excuse about office renovation. To avoid spending a boring evening alone, I invited half a dozen of the officials to join me for dinner at the hotel. They accepted and we spent a pleasant evening together, but I was doubtful about my chances of securing any worthwhile business. Wrong again! Back in London, I had a telephone call a few weeks later, asking me to come to the Bulgarian Embassy where I found one of the officials from Sofia waiting for me. He explained the purpose of his visit to London:

My government has bought a licence to manufacture British fuel injection pumps, but they have not bought details of the manufacturing process. I have been sent here to order manufacturing machinery, but I don't know which machines are needed and where to get them. I wonder if you can help me.

I knew exactly what he needed because the British manufacturer had been one of my customers, so I offered to make a list of the relevant machinery suppliers for him. He looked worried and said:

This is my first trip to England and I am a purely technical man. I do not know much about English commercial terms. If I give you an office with a desk and telephone, would you please arrange for offers to be sent here for me and help me sort them out?

I was delighted to comply with his request and I even negotiated discounts for him. Some of the machinery was obtainable from my regular suppliers and I resisted the temptation to demand introductory commissions from the other suppliers. For many months after my grateful Bulgarian friend returned to Sofia I received further lucrative orders for machinery. When the flow of orders ceased abruptly, I discovered that my important client had been killed in an air crash at Bratislava. At that time, air crashes occurred all too often but, as a frequent flyer, averaging eighty flights per year, I retained the same fatalistic attitude to flying that I had adopted during the war. Unlike the average airline passenger, I never complained about double bookings, delays, diversions and cancelled flights, but I was never entirely happy about the tired appearance of some of the middle-aged commercial pilots. Most of my wartime contemporaries had been in their early twenties!

Flying around behind the Iron Curtain in the ramshackle old Russian planes of Balkan Airlines was a bit scary. The passengers, all of whom were travelling on official business, sat in old-fashioned omnibus seats and nobody used seat belts. People casually strolled about or stood talking with their friends throughout the flights and smoked all the time, even during landings. I once boarded a Balkan Airlines' plane and found that all the seats were occupied. Instead of telling me to disembark, a young black-haired stewardess, with traces of a dark moustache casually told me to go to the back of the plane and sit on my suitcase in the aisle. I thought I might have been more comfortable sitting in the toilet. The girl seemed popular with the male passengers, who laughed and joked with her continually throughout the flight. I guess they were her regular passengers.

Occasionally, unpleasant wartime memories were triggered by unusual incidents on business trips. At about five o'clock one morning we approached Bombay airport in broad daylight. It had been a normal routine flight on Air India until the pilot announced in a singsong Indian accent, 'Ladies and gentleman, we have a small emergency.' I shuddered and my brain seemed to scream silently, 'There is no such thing as a small emergency thousands of feet up in the air without parachutes. Why didn't he explain what had gone wrong?' A steward hurried to the front of the plane brandishing a small screwdriver. On his way past me, I grabbed him by the arm and asked, 'What on earth is wrong with this plane that you can fix with that screwdriver?' He politely explained that, according to the instruments, the nose wheel was not down and locked, so he was going to remove the cover and have a look at it. I remembered that, before every landing, my radio operator had crawled under the flight deck of our wartime Liberator bomber to check by the light of his torch that the nose wheel was securely locked down. Had the aviation industry really made no technical progress since the war? The Indian pilot's voice came over the loudspeakers, 'Ladies and gentlemen, we will now circle for a while over the sea and then make several runs over the airfield before landing'.

The Indian passenger in the next seat, looking as concerned as I felt, kept repeating, 'I think it is very dangerous. I think it is very dangerous.'

I told him, 'The pilot will be jettisoning fuel over the sea as a safety precaution. That is the normal procedure in an emergency.'

My fellow passenger was not listening to me. He was mumbling words in his own language. I thought he might be praying. After half an hour over the sea, we roared repeatedly across the airfield at a height of about 100 feet. Scores of spectators, dressed in what looked like white nightshirts, stood pointing up at us. Half-forgotten newspaper reports of air accidents came crowding into my head. On several recent occasions, when doors flew off airliners, stewardesses were sucked out to fall thousands of feet to their deaths. An American client told me how he heard one young woman's bloodcurdling screams as she tumbled through the air to her death in a nearby field. I tried to think of other things. I surely had not survived crashes and wounds during the war to be killed by Air India in peacetime. Stewards vigorously tightened our seatbelts until we could hardly breathe, placed pillows on our knees and told us to bend forward into the 'crash position'. I looked around for the emergency exits and wondered whether I might have been safer in a cheaper seat near the tail than in first class at the front of the plane.

We made a slow approach and touched down on the runway. As the plane slowed to a stop, I unclenched my teeth. Although the instruments still indicated to the contrary, the nose wheel was safely locked in the down position, so there was no need for the crash tenders and fire engines that stood in readiness. I recalled the appropriate air force sayings, 'Panic over! Only birds and bloody fools fly. Silly bugger, you shouldn't have joined.' I tried to appear unconcerned as my local Indian manager greeted me with the comment, 'Such a terrible loud noise that plane made flying so low over the airfield! I thought something must be wrong with it.'

I told him with forced nonchalance, 'It was just a small emergency.'

My suite of rooms in the splendid Taj Mahal Hotel overlooked the impressive 'Gateway to India'. After the 'small emergency,' I was in need of a stiff drink, and I forgot that alcohol was strictly prohibited in Bombay. Servants were everywhere in the hotel and I absentmindedly asked one of them to direct me to the bar. He said, 'Are you an alcoholic? If you are, you can register at the reception desk and get a stamp in your passport to allow you to purchase alcohol.' Having no wish to be branded as an alcoholic, I settled for a fruit juice instead.

After a stinking hot day, I accepted my local man's invitation to visit his home in the evening. He locked the doors and drew the curtains before hauling a crate of lager from under a divan. Astonished, I said, 'I thought there was supposed to be no alcohol in Bombay.'

He laughed, 'Well officially you cannot get any, but we row out in a dinghy after dark and buy what we need off the ships at anchor in the harbour.'

We settled down to a relaxed session on Danish lager and I said, 'Look what a cheeky street trader gave me as change this afternoon – out-of-date coins with the king's head and the words *Emperor of India* on them.'

My man examined the coins and said, 'They are alright. They are still legal tender.'

I chided him light-heartedly, 'Our king is not your emperor now. You are an independent republic.'

He sighed and shook his head, 'It will be a long time before we can afford to make our own coins. For thirty years of my life, we agitated for the end of British rule and after the war I expected that we would need to keep on protesting for another thirty years, but the British abruptly packed up and left within six months. We were not ready for the sudden change. The situation was absolutely chaotic and now our own government is doing things that we protested about during British rule.'

I was aware that a state of chaos inevitably resulted from hasty British withdrawals from the territories of our vast empire on which it was said that the sun never set.

I thought that an eventual break-up of the Kremlin's empire would most certainly result in utter chaos, but I never expected that I would live long enough to witness such an occurrence. In fact, when a western political commentator asked me in the 1960s, 'How long do you think the communists are likely to remain in control of the eastern bloc?' I answered, 'Possibly a further five hundred years.' The Cold War's political and military adversaries on both sides of the Iron Curtain appeared to accept the insane threat of mutually assured annihilation as the best or only means of preventing the Cold War from heating up. I could foresee no end to that situation.

By the 1970s, I was spending about one third of each year in countries behind the Iron Curtain and in Tito's Socialist Federation. Many British engineering firms were closing down, so I had to seek alternative western suppliers on the continent of Europe and in the United States of America. During my business career I found that, in general, the Germans were the most efficient, and co-operative, suppliers. The Japanese were the most charming and generous clients. The Danes, Swedes and Dutch were the most difficult, and some of my fellow countrymen were the world's most deceitful business people.

During frequent and extensive business tours of the United States I found that, generally speaking, Americans were among the most friendly and hospitable, but naïve and insular, of individuals. Many of them had never had occasion to travel out of their home states and few had heard of the vaunted 'special relationship' with Britain. The vast majority of American families originated from countries outside the British Empire and their only link with England was through their version of the English language. As American-English accents vary throughout the States, I was often thought to be an

American from 'back east'. I explained on such occasions, 'I am from England and I don't mean New England – I mean old England.' Sir Philip, my sometime business partner with his upper-class English accent and strange mannerisms, was never mistaken for an American of any sort. 'Gee, you talk real cute,' they told him.

Thanks to the effect of British tourist advertisements, many Americans viewed England as a quaint little place with Beefeaters and castles – a distant foreign country where Lords, Ladies, Kings, Queens and other strange people dressed themselves up in weird clothes and spoke with peculiar English accents. One summer evening, I took a visiting American client from Seattle on a non-stop tour of the sights of London by taxicab. This was his first visit to London. As we drove from the Houses of Parliament, past Buckingham Palace, he asked me, 'The Dook of Edinburow – is he the King?'

I said, 'No, he is not the King.'

Whereupon he commented, 'He ain't the King, but he's shacking up with the Queen? The King must be real mad.'

We turned into the Mall and sped through Admiralty Arch onto Trafalgar Square. I pointed out Nelson's Column and noticed the back of the cabby's shoulders still shaking as he chuckled over my guest's naïve question about the 'Dook of Edinborow'.

In the mid-1960s, I approached a firm in California and told them that I wanted to buy some of their advanced electronic equipment for shipment directly to my clients behind the Iron Curtain. They told me that, although there was no official embargo, they dared not ship their products to destinations behind the Iron Curtain for fear of upsetting their most important client – NASA; but they agreed to ship the goods to me in England and they did not care what happened to them after that. Several other American firms operated unofficial embargoes on their products.

At one time the Hungarian government asked me to procure for them some large American gear-cutting machines for use in the manufacture of heavy motor vehicle engines. An American firm already supplied that type of machine to Poland, but declined orders from Hungary. I was puzzled by the discrimination until the Hungarian Commercial Attaché suggested a reason, 'There are a lot of influential people of Polish descent in the American administration who are sympathetic to Poland, but they don't care about us.'

My clients behind the Iron Curtain never asked me to supply goods that were subject to official western embargoes, although I assumed that embargoes hindered the manufacture of some of their products. I raised the subject during a meeting with a senior East German official. I said, 'The imposition of western embargoes on certain goods must cause you many problems.'

He replied, 'Your long experience of dealing with us should have taught you that we never buy anything at all from the West unless it is absolutely vital to our economy. And if goods are essential, we simply have to obtain them by some means.'

He gave me no explanation, but I could imagine various simple, though costly, ways of circumventing western embargoes.

For many years I was a frequent visitor to WMW (a German state purchasing organization) in the Soviet sector of Berlin. On fine days I walked there through the Brandenburg Gate. On wet days I tramped up and down the taxi ranks of the western sector trying to persuade one of the drivers to take me to my destination. Most of them refused and I asked one of them if he was afraid of the communists. He said, 'We are not afraid to go into the Soviet sector, but the reason we don't go is simply because our insurance is not valid over there.' Fortunately, money is the most powerful means of persuasion and I usually found a driver who would risk making the trip for an enhanced fee. One day the Stasi, East German security police, and soldiers erected a barbed-wire barrier and checkpoints between the East and West sectors, so that Germans were no longer free to enter and leave East Berlin without authorization. Consequently, some family members and courting couples were isolated from each other. I often saw little groups of tearful people waving handkerchiefs to their relatives on the other side of the barrier. A few people succeeded in scrambling to safety through the wire, and then the East German border guards were ordered to shoot anyone seeking asylum in the West. Before long the notorious Berlin Wall replaced the temporary wire barrier.

During the erection of both the wire and the Wall I could pass unhindered in and out of the Soviet sector by merely showing my British passport to the guards. The erection of the Berlin Wall caused indignant uproar in the western media, but I could see sound economic reasons for it. As a supplier of western capital equipment, an impoverished, under-developed East Berlin was of little use to me and I had wondered how long the East German authorities would allow their best people to leave for highly-paid jobs in the West after they had received an excellent free education in the East. I thought that people should be obliged to remain where they had received their education and training as repayment of their debt to society. I kept such opinions to myself, of course. Each time I crossed over from the rapidly developing western sectors into the depressing Soviet sector of Berlin, I entered a world of grim-faced and deprived people where vast areas of ruined buildings still awaited the first signs of restoration.

East Berlin in the late 1960s reminded me of West Germany in 1950, where hundreds of grief-stricken women and children had waited for hours at the railway stations, hoping to meet men returning from Russian captivity. When trains arrived, the women held up papers showing the names of their missing men in the hope that somebody might have information about them. The Russians had deliberately starved many captured German troops to death and, as only about five per cent survived captivity, most of the women waited at the stations in vain, and they would never know what had happened to their men. All around the railway stations fluttering scraps of paper fixed to walls and railings bore pleas for news of missing families or information about the present whereabouts of bombed-out survivors. It seemed that the whole world was full of misery.

Margit Rytorova, a Czech schoolgirl, was smuggled out of Prague and transported to England by British friends when Nazi troops approached her home town. As soon as she reached the age of seventeen she joined the Royal Air Force and served as a technician on a Canadian bomber squadron. Throughout her war service, she received no news from Czechoslovakia and she was concerned that her father's anti-Nazi views might lead to his arrest. When the war ended she immediately returned to Prague in search of her parents.

She roamed the streets of Prague for days on end, peering into the face of every elderly woman who bore any resemblance to her mother. Sadly, she eventually discovered that both parents had been murdered in a concentration camp. By that time the communists had taken control of the country and she was trapped behind the Iron Curtain. Making the best of the situation, she married a Czech airman who was then sacked from his job at Prague airport and they were both persecuted for the rest of their lives because she had served in the Royal Air Force.

By the time I met her, Margit was an impoverished widow, trying to exist on the meagre amount of money she earned by selling apples from her orchard. She showed me a wartime photograph of herself as an attractive young woman in Royal Air Force uniform. I said, 'What a pity you did not stay in England after the war.' She told me, 'While I was on the Canadian squadron a couple of my boyfriends asked me to marry them, but I told them that I had to return to Czechoslovakia in search of my parents. The communists would not let me out, so I have had to remain here.'

Among the most unfortunate former British Army veterans were the Czechoslovak women who fled to Palestine to avoid persecution by the Germans. Most of them were working as domestic servants when the British opened recruiting offices in the Middle East and the women eagerly joined our Army and saw action during the desert campaign. They qualified for the Africa Star and although they got the ribbon they never got the Star and they never saw Britain. After the war they returned to their homeland to face discrimination and punishment by the communists for serving in the British Army. By the time I discovered them, their numbers had been reduced to only a couple of dozen widows living in deprived circumstances. I never met anyone in Britain who had even heard of them.

During the Second World War most British people had enthusiastically supported the bombing of Germany as the best way to hit back at Hitler. The Allies' policy of massive attacks on civilian targets was hidden from the public and official news bulletins gave the impression that our bombing attacks were made only on military and industrial targets. Our civilians, who were sick of wartime regulations such as strict rationing, for which the Germans were blamed, viewed us flying men with admiration. We were the easily recognizable boys in air force blue who were punishing the perpetrators of actions like the London Blitz. We were popular heroes and the girls swarmed around us like flies around a honey pot. We loved it, but our popularity was short-lived once the shooting stopped.

The war had not been over very long before some people started to regard all wartime bomber crews as merciless killers who were apparently unaffected by the deaths of their unseen victims on the ground thousands of feet below them. Our detractors had not lived in a devastated war zone, as we did in Italy, where we saw the terrible effects of air warfare on the maimed, homeless and starving civilian population. Although we did not actually hear the screams of the dying as we dropped our bombs, their cries will be with some of us for the rest of our days.

During the Cold War, Germany became an important and powerful member of NATO. Pilots of the new Luftwaffe flew American jet planes and trained alongside those of the Royal Air Force. I formed contacts with scores of veterans of the Luftwaffe through their organization, *Gemeinschaft der Jagdflieger*. When the German veterans held a reunion meeting at RAF Coningsby, the home of the Battle of Britain Memorial Flight, they invited me to join them. Some of them had become wealthy retired businessmen who landed at Coningsby in their own private planes. As we laughed and joked together, it seemed ridiculous that as young men we had done our best to kill each other. In wartime, our propaganda-mongers had sought to dehumanize the enemy. Our bomber squadron commander had prefaced details of the night's targets with, 'Gentlemen, another chance to get a crack at the Hun,' and a common wartime saying was, 'The only good German is a dead one', although most British people had never even seen one. Now times had changed, and made a mockery of the efforts of thousands of dead airmen on both sides. I never felt the slightest animosity towards former enemy servicemen who, like me, had done what they were told to do and what seemed right at the time. I was severely wounded while bombing German troops. The enemy soldiers did what they had to do; they hit back and I certainly did not blame them for it. I blamed the people who caused the war and all the consequent suffering. I also hated the thought that it could easily happen again.

From the Luftwaffe veterans I learned that Göring, the head of the Luftwaffe, branded them as cowards after the Battle of Britain. They certainly did not seem like cowards when I encountered them in the air.

Our authorities were just as callous as Göring was. Men who cracked under the strain of air combat were branded with the stigma of LMF (lack of moral fibre); in other words, cowardice. Some Air Ministry psychiatrists even probed family medical histories to find out if any relatives had suffered from mental breakdowns. It was as though they wanted to prove that the airmen had some inherent mental weakness. Some of my colleagues, who simply broke down under the strain of being shot at every night, were reduced to the ranks and sentenced to ten years' penal servitude. Some men were 'rehabilitated', declared fit and returned to flying duties, to die another night. One of our final humiliations came at the end of the war when aircrew flight sergeants were ordered to remove their crowns from their sleeves, and warrant officers were ordered to remove their rank badges and wear only sergeants' stripes while awaiting demobilization. The men had done nothing wrong. The humiliating measure seemed like a punishment for opting to leave the air force rather than signing on for further service.[1] We were widely vilified for actions such as the terrible firestorms of Hamburg and the sickening destruction of Dresden.

When the judges at the Nuremberg trials declared that the plea 'I was just carrying out orders' was not a legitimate defence, it seemed to us that many people thought that the aircrews of our strategic bomber offensive were just as guilty as the Nazi war criminals were. We had obediently carried out the orders of men sheltering safely in their bombproof bunkers and after the war was won, we continued to take the flak. After over 55,000 bomber crewmen were killed in the air, the survivors were callously betrayed and the wounded were treated like malingerers.

It is not surprising that very few bomb-aimers have been willing to talk to civilians about their war service.

Publisher's note:

1 Could it be that the men were returning to substantive rank, i.e the rank to which their service entitled them?